McColl of

THE WILD

ISBN: 978-1-291-96867-5

PublishNation, London
www.publishnation.co.uk

FOREWORD

My brother, Iain McColl, was a very special, gifted Scottish actor. He died on 4th July 2014, aged 59 of Multiple Myeloma. He carried his illness with dignity, bravery and always with humour.

An older brother is someone to look up to and to take advice from. Someone who is always there for you, no matter what, and Iain was certainly always there!

I miss hearing him calling me "Sis" and the laughter we shared, his brown eyes twinkling as he joked.

His greatest wish, towards the end of his life, was to publish his book, not for profit, but to make other people, on the same journey, laugh at his antics.

I made a last promise to Iain that I would do my best to carry out his final wish.

With the assistance of family and friends, I have compiled this story of Iain's life.

Martha (McColl) Brindley.

Acknowledgements

When I promised my brother Iain that I would finish his book for him, little did I realise the mammoth task ahead of me!

It was Iain's wish that the proceeds from the "McColl of the Wild" were to go to 'Friends of the Beatson' charity. He received wonderful care, support and comfort from the staff there and he hoped that by writing this book, other patients would also find some comfort.

My heartfelt thanks go to: Harry Morris, for encouragement and belief in me. Ian Pattison, for setting me on the road, taking time to write a contribution and answering all my questions! John Murtagh, Ross King, Brian Pettifer, Tom Urie, Tony Roper, Gavin Mitchell, Alex Norton for your memories. Colin Gilbert, for his belief in Iain. June Toner, for the laughs and tears as well as the Tommy Cooper photo! John Quinn for his help with publication. Brian Beacom of the Glasgow Herald for his understanding and assistance with publicity. Dr Richard Soutar for the final chapter and support throughout Iain's illness. Staff at the Beatson for their patience and care of Iain. MacMillan staff for help with the endless form filling! My wee brother Donny McColl for all the memories and hugs. My nephew Calum, for the opening chapter. Daughter Cat Gibbons for her support, contribution and faith in me. Cousins Mick and Donny MacNeil for their support and tales of their daft big cousin, also for the lyrics of Iain's favourite song, "Road to Vatersay". Rona Blythe for the wonderful old photo. Joe Greenan, Iain's brother from another mother! Jamie Doherty and his memories, John Stahl, for signing the Equity forms all those years ago! Sonia Scott for giving Iain a chance when the chips were down for him. Kenneth Miller for the aerial view of my childhood homes and for sharing memories of the swing park in Weir Street where Iain dumped me! Thanks to the Glasgow Herald and The Scotsman for permission to reproduce obituaries. Glasgow City Archives for permission to reproduce Weir St photograph. Special thanks to David Morrison at Publish Nation for helping me get this book into print.

To Duncan Watt, my partner, who put up with me during Iain's illness and provided much needed emotional support, helped to look after my dogs, gave me hugs when I needed them, helped with proof reading and was always there quietly in the background. Without you, I would have buckled under the strain. You are amazing and I love you very much.

Last, but not least, to all the Uist people who put up with Iain and me during our childhood and made it so memorable! Auntie Mary Mac Donald of Braeside in Garrynamonie for always being on our side and for having such a big heart! My cousin Dolina Mac Millan for shared memories.
To say "Thank you" is really not enough for all the help I received in the year since Iain died.

If I have forgotten to mention anyone, please accept my deepest apologies.

Any mistakes herein are entirely mine and no offence is intended to anyone.

To all at The Friends of the Beatson, you are wonderful.

The book is dedicated to the memory of my brother Iain and our parents John and Annie McColl.

You are forever in my heart.

Proceeds from this book to be donated to

Beatson Cancer Charity
(Formerly)
Friends of the Beatson Charity

CHARITY NUMBER SCO 44442

My sincere thanks go to all those who purchase this book.

Martha Brindley

Beatson Cancer Charity

If you have bought this book I thank you, the reader, for purchasing it. If you are reading this book without having purchased it please consider a donation, however small, to "The Friends of the Beatson." You are donating to a fantastic charity which benefits the lives of so many people.

The aim of the charity is the provision of practical comfort and support for patients of the Beatson Hospital in Glasgow. It was established by former patients with the encouragement of senior medical staff at the Beatson. It sounds as if they offer a shoulder to cry on and an ear for listening but, anyone who has ever been to the Friends knows that there is so much more offered there.

A range of therapies including hand and foot massage, Reike, Indian head massage, hypnotherapy, hairdressing and chiropody are offered there to all in need. From the moment you walk in the door you are assured of the warmest of welcomes from the staff.

Iain was a regular visitor at the Friends and as I accompanied him to the Clinic and visited him when he was an inpatient, I too enjoyed many a cup of coffee and a chat with the staff. The Friends not only make cancer patients' lives better but also the families of the patients too. Unless you have been there with a family member, it is not easy to understand the toll the illness takes on patients and their families.

Many a time, on my journey with Iain, I experienced difficulty in coping and seeing my brother struggle with his illness. At times like these I would walk along the corridor and pop into the Friends for a coffee and a chat. Sometimes also, a hug would be given and my tears would flow. I cannot express my thanks for the kind words and comfort given to me at this time. Just to say "thank you" is somehow not enough. I hope by completing this book for Iain, I find within me the means, not only to carry out my promise to him, but also give back something to the Friends in thanks for everything they did for Iain and me.

I have gifted to Friends of the Beatson, a copy of this book and a stone from Garrynamonie Machair on South Uist. The final stage of the journey and Iain's resting place. It was where he was most at peace and where he wished to be laid to rest.

My young nephew Calum, my Brother Donny's youngest son, has the honour of writing the opening chapter.

Calum was 8 years old at the time of writing his memories of Iain.

Calum McColl

Uncle Iain always made me laugh. He gave me great Christmas presents too, my favourite was a football table, and he was my favourite Uncle.

He was an actor and he always acted goofy which was fun. He knew good "Knock Knock" and "Doctor" jokes and he was always very funny.

50 words worthy of its own chapter Calum!

Iain loved Calum very much. I am sure he would have been very proud of Calum for taking the time to write a wee bit about his Uncle.

Way to go wee guy!

Catherine Gibbons (Iain's Niece & God Daughter)

My daughter was the firstborn Grandchild and my parents were very proud of her, as I am also. She has grown up to be a very remarkable young lady. She has achieved so much in her life and her Grandparents would be very proud of her achievements.

Iain was the obvious choice, when she was born, to be her Godfather and he was delighted when I asked him if he would carry out the role.

He always remembered her birthdays and often talked about her when I was accompanying him for his chemotherapy.

Iain was a very proud Uncle.

Catherine's memories.

Finding where to begin to talk about my Uncle Iain is a difficult task! I have been so lucky and blessed to have grown up surrounded by strong influential characters and Iain McColl, aka "The Godfather", was definitely one of them.

My earliest memory of a strong influential character was my Granddad John, Iain's Dad, a Glaswegian man who sat me on his lap and fed me Maltesers from a box at the age of 2. I genuinely do remember this although he passed away not long after that.
My earliest memory of my Uncle Iain was when I was roughly 4 years old. Iain was tickling me and I was pinned down on my back by one huge strong hand, when I was in my Gran's house, and I literally could not breathe for laughing so hard.

My Gran was an amazing woman and I still miss her. I can still hear her infectious laugh and Gaelic chatter on the phone to her Sister Morag. I spent almost every weekend at my Grans and usually it was alternate weekends with my cousins, Iain's children, who I shared a toy box with, leaving notes for my cousin week about when we didn't see each other. I look back over all my memories with great fondness.

As a tribute to Iain, I have chosen to run in the Loch Ness Marathon in September 2014. The money raised from sponsorship is for the Friends of the Beatson. Iain received so much care and support at the Friends and I often heard my Mum say how kind they were to her when she was at the Beatson with Iain. If not for this support, I know Mum would have struggled to cope emotionally as her brother's health slowly deteriorated.
A copy of this book will be placed in the Friends as a lasting legacy to my amazing Uncle, Iain McColl.

I never knew him as being different or suffering from Bipolar disorder, even from that age, he was always just Uncle Iain. He was always the one who was full of fun and the life and soul of any party or family do. Everyone loved him in our family and would be delighted when he appeared lighting up anywhere with his presence and making the kids laugh with his antics.

He was the one who taught me about rubbing a balloon on your head and sticking it to your jumper and always signed any birthday card or Christmas card, "the Godfather" this wasn't because he thought he was the God father (or maybe he did!) but because he was mine and I know, that when I took my Communion and Confirmation after my Dads passing, he was there and was a very proud Godfather. In spite of being so ill at that stage he sat through the 4 hour mass just to be there and support me, I was lucky to have him as such a support.

Not that my Uncle Iain was an angel by any means. I do have a memory, when I must have been 6 years old, of being in the back seat of an old Escort or similar with my 2 Uncles Iain and Donny hurtling over country roads as fast as they could and also going rabbit shooting at about the same age when he lived in Tighnabruaich. He would swing me in the middle of my Dad and him with one hand to "1 2 3 Weeeee" with a shotgun and rabbits in the other. This was at his home in Argyll and I have many fond memories of staying there. I was introduced to" Bob" the horse and when asking how to steer the horse my Uncle Iain said "pull right for right and left for left" and I was left to it!

I also remember Squash the dog having pups up the bark of a fallen down tree and my Uncle Iain pulling them out with a Shepherds' crook as my cousins and I carried them back to the house, later I chose one as a pet. Another fond memory is of staying at Aunt Mary's house in South Uist at the age of 16 with my Gran. We went on holiday and my best friend came with us, we looked for mischief and we certainly found it! Just like my Mum and Uncle Iain had done years before us!

One day when Iain was nearing the end, my Mum phoned me. She was upset and I suggested playing the Vatersay boys for Iain, like the Highland Music we played for Gran in hospital, I think he'd have liked it.

One thing is for sure my Uncle Iain never judged me for what I do and I didn't judge him. He was a complex character and one who was hard to get to know or get close to but what I do know is that whenever I did spend time in his company, at a family do for example, he would be making sure I was ok by keeping an eye on me, If I caught him, he always gave me a wee wink that said a million words without saying any. It's hard to explain but he was saying I'm watching you, I love you and I'm making sure you're ok with just a wink.

This picture is a favourite of mine. My Dad and my Uncle on his wedding day, I like to think that they're like that right now looking down over us. They both had their troubles but they were my Dad and Uncle and nothing changes the love I had for them.

This photo is from a time I remember with fondness.
My Grandmother Annie McColl, my Mum Martha and 2 of
Iain's children.

Martha's memories of Early Years

Iain's story began on 27th January 1954 when he was born in Lennox Castle Hospital.

Our mother, Anne and father John were delighted with the arrival of their first child and took him home to 117 Weir Street in Kinning Park, Glasgow. It was a one room and kitchen, single end, complete with toilet in the "close" near to the River Clyde and the bustling docks. Our mother was an excellent homemaker and soon made the tiny house comfortable. She sourced two wooden boxes, used for transporting oranges, covered them with hand embroidered table cloths and they became two lovely wee tables!

At that time our father was an Insurance Agent for Prudential. He was a hard working man, who hailed from Govan and always strived to better himself and provide for his family. He ruled with a rod of iron and woe betides anyone who came across him.

Iain was an easygoing baby and 16 months later on May 30th 1955, I came along to shatter his existence! He got fed up one day with my crying and pushed the pram, with me wrapped up in it, along to the park at the bottom of Weir St and promptly left me there beneath the chute. Iain ran home and told my mother that I was in the park playing on the chute! Luckily for me, a kindly lady found me and brought me up Weir St. Shouting "who lost a wean?"

Mother and child were quickly reunited and I think that was the first time Iain got a thrashing from our father. He was three years old then.

Weir St Park: where Iain abandoned me at age 2

Brother and Sister always had a strong love for each other but we would argue constantly over who played with what toys! Iain had a wee three wheeler bike for Christmas one year. I think he was five years old and I was four. I had a lovely pram and a beautiful doll which I christened Penelope. Iain promptly drew on the doll's face in blue ink and cut its hair off. He then took my pram and bounced it off a lamppost outside the house, buckling a wheel. It limped along like a dodgy supermarket trolley for a few months before Mum put it in the midden outside the back door of our house.

Iain was ever resourceful and he climbed into the midden, claiming it back to take the wheels off it and make a "bogey" for us to ride on. This consisted of a plank of wood, wheels at both sides and a piece of old washing line to steer it with. The various materials were scavenged from bins and back courts around Weir Street. If you wanted to put the brake on, you merely stuck both feet firmly on the ground and hoped that you would grind to a halt without breaking your ankles!

I waited patiently for my revenge and when Iain went to school a few days later, I took his bike and rammed it into the same lamppost! The front wheel was well and truly buckled and Iain was not a happy boy! We called it quits at that. Justice was sweet.

Another favourite pastime of Iain's was playing marbles in the street. There was a culture in Glasgow back then for children to play outdoors in the street where you lived. Iain enjoyed playing in the gutter, rolling his shiny coloured marbles into the metal grate which was full of small, marble sizes holes! He often robbed me of my prized coloured, glass ball, or "Jorries" as we called them. I never won any of his so I guess he had a better eye for that kind of game than his Sister had, but I think he always cheated!

There was a shop opposite our house called Irish Maggie's where Mum would often send me for a wee "message "or two. On one occasion she asked me to get her some potatoes and off I toddled across the street, clutching a piece of paper and some money. Maggie duly read the note and dropped some potatoes into the bag Mum gave me. It was an old holdall which was used to put the vegetables in. No plastic carrier bags in 1960!

As I left the shop, I tripped on the edge of the kerb and the potatoes went shooting off in all directions. I skinned my knee but hobbled across to the house where I enlightened Mum about my accident. She was only worried about the lost potatoes and went flying out to round them up from all corners of the street. Money was tight for her and she could ill afford to lose our dinner. When she returned, I had my knees scrubbed with carbolic soap and bathed in salt water! What a brilliant piece of first aid carried out by a woman who would go on to become a nursing assistant in her later years.

Next to our house was a builder's yard, Currie's I think it was called, on a cold day Mum would make a huge pot of soup. She always took some in to the yard for the watchman, who always received it with grateful thanks. The lovely old chap lived close to our Grandmother's house in Penilee and we knew him well. In return for this act of kindness, we were the only children allowed to play in the yard, which was covered over, like a huge shed. Heaps of sand and other building materials were our playthings on wet days. Health and Safety would have been all over it like a rash if it was today! Iain always took his "Dinky" cars in to play with. He would run up to the top of the piles of sand until one day the heap started to slide slowly down, burying Iain underneath it. I ran screaming to the watchman and then to my Mum for help. Iain was pulled free from the pile but his only concern was that his toy cars were lost underneath. He never realised what a close encounter with death he had that day.

That was the first time I told Iain his wee Sis had saved his life.

We both got smacked that day! No surprise there then eh?

My poor mother never had her sorrows to seek with her two wayward children and it was not long before we were in the wars again. In the back court was a six foot high wall, or dike as we kids called it. We liked nothing better than to climb up the wall and run along the top playing Cowboys and Indians shouting our wee heads off. One day Iain overbalanced in pursuit of me and tumbled to the ground. I looked down and saw Iain motionless in the dirt and screamed loudly for help. My cries attracted the attention of a passing man and woman who came to our assistance. The woman lifted me down and took me home to inform Mum what had happened. Mum ran across the back court to Iain and the lady ran to a nearby phone box to call an ambulance. Iain was carted off to hospital. One fractured skull later and the headlines in the Evening Citizen were;

"Cowboy Iain takes a fall".

So began Iain's on off love affair with the media!

Iain always said I saved his life twice.

What a brother to grow up with. He always went at double speed through his childhood and that continued as he grew up into his teenage years and adulthood.

We both had a fascination with Westerns when we were children and that started Iain's thoughts of being an actor.
Every Saturday we went to the matinee at the cinema called the Korky. At least we called it that, I think it was in Houston Street. Later on we went to one in Cornwall Street. Iain would sneak in

the side door without paying while I stood in the queue distracting the usher; we bought ice cream with the money saved. We loved John Wayne and Gary Cooper and ran home whooping and hollering like mad, re-enacting the big screen antics of our favourite actors. I was always fascinated with Calamity Jane and wanted nothing more than to drive a stagecoach with six horses through the American West with Iain riding shotgun! Thus began my lifelong love of horses.

Iain went to school but hated the whole experience of discipline and learning. My father taught him how to play various card games and he turned this to good use by teaching other boys and making extra pocket money from playing Poker and cribbage. He spent more time playing cards than learning maths, history and geography!

He had a great teacher, a male who shall remain nameless, and Iain really looked up to him. This teacher enjoyed a wee cigarette or two, which frequently got him into bother!

Iain was sent into the corridor one day, while the teacher lit up a cigarette. His role being, that if the head teacher came in sight, Iain was to go back into class and warn the teacher of her impending arrival. This Iain did and the cigarette was duly snuffed out and placed in the teacher's pocket but not fully extinguished!

Head teacher entered the classroom, asked why the boy, Iain, was in the corridor and was informed by the teacher that he had been cheeky in class!! Iain was given the belt and took his "punishment" without a word of complaint but then he noticed smoke coming from the teacher's pocket. He kept quiet about this until the teacher's leg was burning and calmly said" I would have told you if you weren't too busy belting me".

The teacher was then summoned to the office by the Head but we never learned the outcome of the meeting between them!

Iain would often truant from Our Lady and St Margaret's school and on these occasions would ask me at going home time, what lessons I had in school that day. When Mum asked him what he learned, he would cheerfully repeat what I told him!

I soon learned to blackmail him for a penny or two to buy my silence!

On wet weather days, Iain and I would play games in the house on Watt Street. A favourite one was Hide and Seek. Now, you may not think there would be many places to hide in a two bedroom tenement flat two stories up but we were nothing if not resourceful! It was my turn to hide and I scampered off into our bedroom to look for a suitable hidey hole. I decided that the huge, mahogany wardrobe, complete with double doors and a mirror in the middle would do just fine. I clambered in and squeezed in beside the clothes, waiting patiently for Iain to come looking for me. He duly took his time and I got fed up waiting for him. I leaned too far forward and the wardrobe fell with a bang, face down trapping me inside it. I screamed out loud and the next thing I knew was Mum pushing the wardrobe over to release me from its confines. Mum dragged me out, shook me and skelped me on the backside. I had her old fur, fox stole wrapped around my neck and my ears were ringing! The mirror was smashed to pieces and Iain was laughing like a hyena at my predicament.

I think Iain won that round then!

School years began for me in 1960, and on my first day at Our Lady and St Margaret's school in Stanley Street, Iain was asked to bring me home when school was over for the day. Iain, however, had other ideas and promptly ran off, leaving me to make my own way back home. I remember it being quite a foggy day and visibility was very poor. I made my way along Paisley Road West trying to follow the lamp posts on the pavement at the edge of the road. I promptly walked into one and fell on my backside, ending up with a black eye and a bruised forehead! I told my Mum that I had fallen over, but I never grassed Iain for running off and leaving me. It was just lucky that I knew the way back to Weir Street as he clearly had no intentions of ever waiting for his Sister!

One of our favourite pastimes was tracing drawings on to paper and colouring them in. We always received crayons and pencils at Christmas from our parents. Now, in those days we never had any spare money to buy proper tracing paper so we had to improvise! We would go to the school toilets and take a couple of sheets of toilet paper; it was the old shiny stuff that didn't work for the intended purpose; fold them carefully and put them on the waistband of our knickers. We would rustle all the way home after school and then release our bounty of the day! Tracing paper with "Izal" printed in green on the corner. Whoopee! Our ready made entertainment for the evening, never mind the fact that our toilet was outside in the close and we never had toilet paper anyway, only torn up newspapers!

I was returning home one Sunday afternoon after playing with a friend and, as I entered the common close, I noticed a young local boy standing in the rear entrance to the close. There was a door to the left which was the back door of Val's Dairy, the shop next to our close. This door was open and the lad, he was about 14 or so, told me to keep moving and say nothing about this to anyone. The dairy was normally closed on Sundays. I ran up the stairs and dutifully informed Mum and Dad that a big boy was breaking in to the shop. My Dad ran downstairs but the boy had gone. In those days we had no phone in the house but I was sent to Pollok Street to the blue Police box and reported the incident.

The Police arrived and I told my tale, giving them the name of the lad who had been there. He was arrested and charged with the burglary but was free to go until the trial. This did not bode well for me as when I left school a few days later, the bold boy was waiting and followed me home. Luckily for me I met up with Iain and his friends and I got home safely.

I received a reward of 7s and 6p in savings stamps for my honesty! That's 37p in today's climate.

Two Police officers delivered my reward, a man and a woman.
I knew then that when I was grown up I would join the Police. That is what I did when I turned 18 years of age but at age 14, I walked into the old Glasgow Police headquarters in St Andrew's Street and asked the Sergeant behind the desk for an application form! He handed one to me and told me to practice filling it in and return with it when I was 18! I kept that form for years until it was time for me to apply in the proper manner.

We roamed the streets of Kinning Park every day after school and at the weekends. One of our favourite capers was to run down to the Clyde Ferry at Shearer Street. Straight down the slipway and dive on just as it was leaving the mooring. It was free to get on but we received an ear bashing from the ferryman for our troubles. We would gaze along the busy river, watching the various ships of all sizes, until we got to the other side at the Broomielaw. Once we jumped off the ferry, Iain would run along the road shouting
"Ye cannae catch me Martha, am too fast for you."
I never could keep up with him and he would be at the next ferry stop long before me. We always came back over on a different boat, usually from Govan and ran along Paisley Road back home.

Health and Safety were nowhere to be seen in the 1960's and it is a miracle that we managed to survive our escapades.

Another favourite game was to cadge a "hudgie" on the back of the coalman's cart. I would distract the man asking questions about Freddie, his Clydesdale horse, and Iain would hang on the back of the cart as he trundled along the street. We later graduated to hanging off the back of the open buses as they crawled along in the fog which was so common at that time in Glasgow.

Great places to play around in those days were the huge sheds along the docks. In those days the Clyde was a very busy river. The sheds stretched all the way from Govan to Paisley Road. Hundreds of men were employed there at that time sorting out all the goods which were unloaded from ships which had sailed to Glasgow from all over the world. We would watch all the unloading of the huge ships along the quay and the efforts of the men at work. Often we would find a trophy to take home and on one occasion Iain found a banana, a rare treat in those days. Well, not to be undone, I promptly went round all the Dockers until one took pity on me and poured some sugar into my cupped hands. I ran home like a cat with two tails to my mother. That evening we watched our wee black and white television eating a banana sandwich with sugar! What a treat indeed.

Our best night of the week was when Rawhide was on television, but Bonanza was a close second. We loved the antics of the Cartwright family, especially Hoss.
My mother would buy a few cream cookies from the City Bakeries and we had a wee feast watching Cowboys in a far away land. We believed everything we watched on the television and were typical innocent children of our generation. This was, along with the Saturday Cinema visits the start of Iain's fascination with Westerns and thus led on to his dream of becoming an actor.

In common with most Glasgow "weans" in those days, Iain and I enjoyed exploring our locality, raiding the bins and searching for old and broken toys to play with. One favourite bin was at the rear of the café on Paisley Road, opposite the old Kingston Halls. You could find old window displays and fake sweeties wrapped up in shiny, coloured paper. What a treasure trove that was. We spent many days playing at shops on the pavement outside 27 Watt Street.

If we discovered anything of use then that particular bin was labelled "the lucky midden".

There was a newsagent on the opposite side of Watt St, a barber shop called Selby's and another shop on the corner called Parlane's. The barber went on to become a local councillor, in Govan, I think.

One Saturday evening, our parents put us to our beds and then went to a neighbour across the landing from us. Now, Mum waited a suitable time until she thought we were sleeping but as soon as she went out the door, up we got and went through to their bedroom, which overlooked Watt Street. At the bottom of the close was Jimmy's Bar. We raised the window up and had a lean out, common practice back then, to watch the customers leaving the pub at 10pm closing time. People were milling about and chatting when Iain decided to have a bit of fun. He nipped through to the kitchen and lifted the teapot, which contained dregs of loose tea. He topped it up with water and brought it back through to the bedroom. "Right, lets drown somebody", he shouts to me. Unfortunately, for them, a man and woman were standing underneath the window chatting and Iain decided that they were his prey!

He poured the cold tea out on top of them and then closed the window. He bolted to the kitchen, replaced the teapot and we dived back into our beds.

A couple of minutes later, a knock on the door and a woman was shouting "Get out of there. I know you are in".

We pretended to be asleep under the covers, trying to suppress our laughter and the next thing, Mum opens the door. She tells the woman her children are sleeping and it could not have been them who did the dirty deed.

The woman stamps off down the stairs in a temper and Mum returns to our bedroom. She pulled the blankets off our beds, removed her slipper and promptly smacked our backsides. Iain and I are doubled up laughing and Mum is not amused!

"Don't bring shame to my door again you hooligans". She shouts at us and then returned to the neighbours!

On special occasions, we would go into the café, and buy ice cream mixed in a tall glass mixed with lemonade. We had to save up a few empty "ginger" bottles, to get their deposits and some pocket money to pay for this treat! There were booths in the café with benches in and we thought we were grown up sitting there sipping our drinks!

We would wait patiently for our Dad to finish his bottle of "Radiant" orange juice so that we could take the bottle to the café and get the deposit back! Happy days indeed.

We grew into our teens and moved from Watt Street to Pollok in 1969 to a bigger house which had 3 bedrooms, a bathroom and a garden. What a luxury it was as Iain and I no longer had to share a bedroom. The worst part about sharing with Iain was, I also had to share with his beloved doos! The constant billing and cooing would drive me insane and keep me awake at nights. Iain, however, slept through it all.

He had fantastic times flying his birds from our tenement window and was only disappointed if one of the birds failed to return home or was captured by a rival "doo man". Payback was sweet, of course, if he caught another man's bird.

We had a neighbour across the landing, Mary Mac Innes, a great friend of Mum's and also from Uist.

Iain went to her door one day and asked her if she could keep two pigeons for him for a short time. Mary agreed and took in the birds for Iain. A little later that day, two Police officers arrived at our door and asked Mum if Iain had any extra pigeons in his doocat. Mum duly checked and informed them that there were no extra birds in the house. They left the scene empty handed and Iain claimed the birds back from Mary who was suitably affronted at harbouring stolen goods! Iain was well warned not to catch any more pigeons belonging to other people and never to bring the Police to the door again.

That warning fell on very deaf ears!

The move to Pollok marked another chapter in our lives and we had much more freedom and new places to explore.

My Mum's Sister, Morag MacNeil, lived across the road from us and we had great times playing with our 7 cousins. Most days, after school, we gravitated across the road to our Aunt's house and we were always made to feel welcome. Iain would be off with Donny and Mick on their bikes and I would hang around with Katie and Janette.

When Iain was in his late teens, he had a job as a "bouncer" in a disco at Sauchiehall Street in Glasgow. You had to be 21 years old to get entry but Iain always got my friend Fiona Dundas and myself in for free. The disco was called "The Revolution" and entry was by way of a flight of stairs leading up from the street. Any unsavoury characters were promptly dispatched by the scruff of their necks down the stairs. It was great getting in without payment but not so good having your brother watch who you were dancing with! Woe betides any amorous suitor who pestered Iain's sister!

After the disco was over, Fiona and I would walk to George Square for the late night bus back to Pollok. This was an hourly service and depending on our arrival time, we would often have to wait some time for the bus to arrive. We were frequent visitors to the "soup kitchen", a mobile van which fed the city's homeless population, and in return for a cup of hot soup, would share our cigarettes with the homeless people who congregated there.

The craze at that time was for guys to dress up like extras from "The Clockwork Orange" film, which had been released around this era. Iain left the disco after his work one Saturday evening and as he entered Sauchiehall Street, six young men in Clockwork Orange garb, complete with large black umbrellas, chased him along the street towards Bath Street. It later transpired that Iain had refused them entry to the Revolution and this was payback time!

Now, Iain was never scared of a fight in his young days but six against one was a bit intimidating, even for Iain Mc Coll!

After running for a couple of minutes, Iain decided to stop, turn round and charge his attackers like a maniac, screaming abuse as he went. His strategy worked and four of the young men turned tail and bolted in the opposite direction. The other two stopped in mid flight and wielded their black umbrellas at Iain. Not to be outdone, Iain put his hand in his inside pocket, as if to pull out a weapon, and said:

"My dad's fae Govan and he taught me how to fight. Do you really want to see what I'm carrying or do you want to join your four cowardly mates?"

The remaining two men decided not to cross this mad man and walked away!

Iain was relieved at their decision for he never had anything in his pocket and just made the whole thing up. He was a good actor even at that point in his life and it certainly got him out of trouble that evening.

One night, when Iain was 20 years old, my Dad received a telephone call around 1am, from a Police officer in Castlemilk, informing him that Iain was in custody. I was in the Police by then and Mum woke me up. I drove Dad to Castlemilk in my fiancé's old Austin Cambridge car to pick up the wayward son. I was not best pleased as that day I was on early shift at 7am. We were informed by the officer that Iain had been charged with a breach of the peace. He had been outside the Doune Castle pub on Kilmarnock Road and been refused entry by a doorman, due to having consumed an excess of alcohol. Iain was having none of that as his friends and cousin had been allowed entry.
The bold boy picked up a dustbin from the kerb and launched it in the door of the pub! Now, any sane person would have scarpered at this point but not our Iain. He sat on the pavement and waited for the law to arrive in order to state his case. He obviously failed in his efforts, was apprehended and duly charged.

I don't know which was worse for Iain that night. Being charged with an offence or having to listen to his Sister berating him all the way home!
"Martha," he said, "I would rather be locked up for the night than listen to you raving on about bins and pubs!"

I went off to work the next day, not best pleased at having my sleep disturbed and when I returned home at 3pm, Iain was just getting out of his bed. Not a word of apology passed his lips, he did, however, ask for a loan of £5 to go out for a drink that night!

To be fair to Iain, he never asked me again to get him out of trouble and always took his punishment.

He was a fantastic big brother to grow up with and always led me into mischief as well as looking out for me.

Iain went off to work in Kuwait, not long after this, with our Dad and the house was much quieter when they were away. We missed them both very much and Mum, Donny and I always looked forward to them coming home on leave with tales of their travels.

Our first family photograph in 1958
This was taken in a studio on Paisley Road near to where we
stayed. Iain is wearing the Fair Isle jumper he gave to the
ragman.
I don't know what my Mum was thinking with the hairstyles!

Baby Iain and Mum in South Uist 1954

Aerial view of Weir St and Watt St.: Our childhood homes.

Iain's own Tale
Genesis

In the beginning God created South Uist, the beautiful island in the Outer Hebrides of Scotland, where my dear mother Anne MacDonald was born. She was one of nine to Donald MacDonald and Kate Steele of Garrynamonie, my "Heiland" Grandparents.

Life was busy on a working croft with ploughing, potato planting, peat cutting, hay making, sheep shearing, cattle droving and fishing......and if you had any spare time you could always feed the chickens or something!

Although life was all hard work, in pre World War 2 years they fared better than most during the 1930's depression. With plenty of fish, potatoes, meat, vegetables, eggs, milk, crowdie, home baked scones on the table. Aaah....the good life right enough.
In fact when war came along, the only ration they were affected by was the lack of whisky!
The blessed **Uisge Beatha** or "Water of Life" for those readers who don't speak the two spokes.
Yes, the lack of whisky in those bleak times amounted to a national disaster of apocalyptic proportions. How dark it is before the dawn.

Another disaster was about to unfold. On 5th February1941, the great ship SS Politician ran aground on rocks off the Island of Eriskay, between Eriskay and South Uist. The ship was carrying 28,000 cases of whisky bound for Jamaica and New Orleans into the hands of Frank Costello and Lucky Luciano mafia crime families. Luciano was not so lucky this time, however, as the islanders celebrated long and hard at this redistribution of wealth. They regarded this disaster as an act of God and thought it was their right to take custody of as much of this bounty as they could before the Customs and Police did!

The local Customs officer, Charles McColl, no relation, had an altogether different view of the proceedings as no duty had been paid on the whisky and this was a loss to the public purse.

Now. It just so happened that my Grandfather, Donald MacDonald, had a wee boat. A small wooden clinker build dinghy, maybe 12 feet or so, which he normally used for fishing for Mackerel. The boat was ideal for robbing the "Polly" of her load as she could hold 50 cases or more of the God sent nectar plus two men. My Uncles, Angus James MacDonald and John Steele who was nicknamed Long John Silver as he towered about 6ft 3inches were eager to help.

The arrangement was that Long John and Angus would take the boat over the Sound of Eriskay to the Polly, as she became known. Long John would transfer cases of whisky by rope down to Angus in the dinghy. He would untie them and stack the boxes, allowing the rope to go back to Long John for more. They would then row round to the shore of Garrynamonie beach where my Grandfather would meet them with horse and cart waiting to transfer the bounty and take it home to the croft.

Whisky was buried on the shore, under giant haystacks in the yard and in the babies cradle! (My Aunt Patricia to be precise)

The deal was a case for each man on the boat and an extra case for the boat owner, Grandfather. They probably had over a hundred cases in the stack yard alone.

Oh how I wish I had been around in those days!

High Fiddly Dee. A pirate's life for me!!

Charles McColl was furious and whipped up such a furore that the local Police had to act. Villages were raided and crofts turned upside down. Bottles were hidden all over the island or simply drunk in order to hide the evidence!

My two Uncles were eventually caught. Long John received 30 days sewing mailbags in Inverness gaol and Angus was fined £5, a lot of money in those days, as he was too young to be imprisoned. Other men were imprisoned in Inverness and Peterhead

My mother and her Sister, my dear Aunt Morag, buried bottles in the family peat bogs, after sampling some themselves. They would then ride home and promptly forgot where the bottles were buried. The whereabouts remain a mystery to this day!

Mmm...I wonder if anyone has invented a whisky detector-I would buy one quick!

Whisky was not the only prize on the "Polly". There were bicycles, in kit form, bedding, plumbing, furniture, motor parts, food as well as Jamaican banknotes and ten shilling notes. Much of this disappeared but some currency turned up in banks all over the world. Local children were found playing with the banknotes but the wily islanders never gave anything away.

I can just imagine Angus and Long John going to Polachar Inn and ordering whisky, offering to pay with handfuls of Jamaican currency just for a laugh!

McColl, meanwhile, estimated that the islanders had purloined over 24,000 cases of whisky and to make sure there was no more looting, applied for permission to dynamite the boat and explode her hull. The islanders watched this with horror and Angus John Campbell commented.

"Dynamiting whisky. You wouldn't think there were men in the world as crazy as that".

Meanwhile, Donald Hector Mc Neil, our next door neighbour in Garrynamonie, had written a play based on those local events. My Mum, Annie MacDonald, played a young girl discovering "Polly" bottles on the beach, or Machair. She had to rush home and tell the family of the good fortune.

Art mirrors reality and it played to sell out crowds in the local halls.

Mum was a bit of a dark horse and only shared this with me in later life.

That's where my flair for theatre came from-it's in the blood!!

It was against this background of colour and characters, that my mother, along with many others, left for Glasgow after the war to seek work in the big city.

My mother had a wicked sense of humour also and had a wonderful ability to laugh at herself.

I loved her very much. She was always there for me, despite my crazy antics and flare for getting into trouble. What a wonderful character she was. She was also good at impersonations and must have passed her talent on to me.

I am sure I caused her bucketfuls of grief over the years but never once did she fail to support my dream of becoming an actor.

I know she was very proud of my achievements on stage but not so pleased with my entire off screen brushes with the law!

Many a time she read me the riot act about my behaviour, despite the fact that I was a grown man with a family of three children.

"Don't make your children ashamed of you." She said in her lovely lilting accent.

Maybe they were and maybe they were not? Who is to say?

Exodus

Arriving on the Paisley Road on Glasgow's South Side, or "Sooside", Anne soon found work on the tram cars as a conductress, or "clippie" collecting fares with her big leather bag and ticket machine.

This is where she met John McColl, a big macho guy from Govan, who was later to become her husband. John was the driver of the tram.

I once asked Mum what she liked about Dad and she told me that after her shift, when she went to pay in the fare money, the other drivers would offer to help her count all the coins. She was always short and never realised that the drivers were exploiting her Highland naivety and robbing her. When she was teamed up with big John, her money was correct and after they started going out together, they never had any more problems with the cash! An honest man my Dad.

Thus I was born in Lennox Castle hospital on 27th January, 1954. We lived in a ground floor single end tenement flat, with back and front doors, at 117 Weir St, Kinning Park, Glasgow. Today, it is the site of Harry Ramsden's fish and chip restaurant near to the Kingston Bridge.

Mum and Dad had, by then, left the employment at Glasgow Corporation Transport. Dad found employment as a window cleaner and then as an insurance agent for Pearl and Prudential insurers.

Dad's next course of employment was the Govan shipyards and then on to scaffolding. He was a wonderful man who always strived to better himself and provide for his family.

My wee Sister, Martha, was born on 30th May, 1955 in our house in Weir St. I called her "Mana," as I couldn't get my tongue round the letter "r" in her name.

She was delivered by a neighbour, acting as midwife and when Dad came home from work my Mum was up on her feet and making his dinner as usual! These Highland women were made of tough stuff. No lying around for them when men had to be fed.

Mum would put Martha in her pram and tie the handle to the window with a length of string. I soon learned to untie this and one day I got fed up listening to the baby crying, untied the string and pushed the pram down Weir Street to the local swing park. I could barely see over the high pram but arrived there safely and promptly left baby and pram parked under the chute. Luckily for me, a wee wifey took the pram back up the street shouting merrily "who lost a wean?" I could not repeat what my Mum said to me when she discovered the pram had disappeared!! Suffice to say that I had a red backside that night.

I loved the evenings at home watching our black and white television set and my favourite programmes, Westerns. Best of all was Rawhide, which starred Eric Fleming as Gill Favor the trail boss and Clint Eastwood as Rowdy Yates his sidekick.

Mum would buy a few cream cakes and sweeties from the wee shop across the street. It was owned by "Irish Maggie", we never called her anything else! I and my young Sister Martha would settle in to watch cowboys and Indians or Native Americans to the modern pc elect!

Dad would switch off the light and it was like being in the cinema! A night out at the pictures-the pictures without leaving the house. Sheer escapism!

Sadly, Eric Fleming drowned whilst filming a stunt that went horribly wrong. I too, whilst no doubt emulating Clint Eastwood, narrowly escaped death in the Cowboy Iain stunt featured in the

Evening Citizen newspaper. This led to me first hitting the headlines in 1958.

Meanwhile, back at the ranch, Mum was knitting beautiful Fairisle sweaters, socks, gloves, balaclavas and Arran sweaters for the summer holidays in Uist. Yes, she was a great knitter, my Mum. I remember when the "ragman" came to our street with a horse and cart blowing his bugle to alert people of his presence. He would shout "toys for rags" at the top of his voice and could be heard several streets away. In exchange for rags he would give a balloon or cheap trinket, usually made in Hong Kong.

Well, one day, on hearing the familiar bugle and shout roll up call, I grabbed my Dad's only suit and rushed along the street to see what I could get.

I handed the suit to the ragman and pulled off my Fairisle sweater which Mum had knitted. Martha was running along behind shouting at me to stop but I just ignored her efforts. She was always the sensible one! The ragman handed me a balloon on a length of string and I set off back home.

On arriving home, Mum, having realised what I did, grabbed me by the hand and marched me out clutching the offending balloon. We caught up with the ragman in Pollok Street and Mum read the Riot Act to the poor businessman for accepting garments which were clearly not rags! I remember her saying

"You better pray I don't tell big John when he gets home. He will stuff that balloon up your bahookie and rap that bugle round your blooming neck."

Mum swore with graphic eloquence, which never sounded like swearing in her lilting Hebridean accent! She grabbed the suit and jumper off the cart, clouted me round the ear and marched me back home.

I was well warned not to tell Dad about the exploits that day, or Mum said there would be a murder in the street when the ragman returned the following week.

My primary school days were spent in Our Lady and St Margaret's Primary School in Kinning Park.

I never enjoyed school very much but one teacher stood out. My music teacher, Miss Edie, lived in a big house in Maxwell Park, Glasgow. This was a very salubrious area in those days. She was a cat lover and I visited her house on Saturday mornings for music tuition. I spent the time counting all her stray cats instead of concentrating on my music! Poor Miss Edie could not understand why I never wanted to sing;
"Oh For the Wings of A Dove!"

I remember her being away on holiday once and my mum had the job of going to the house and feeding the cats. I spent my time chasing them round the garden and my mum shouting at me to: "Leave them alone Iain".

I much preferred "dogging" school and playing cards in the street with my pals.

Schoolboy Iain circa 1967

I don't remember when I crossed that line, but cross that line
I did.

From caterpillar to butterfly in a second.
From boy to man in a moment, a blink of an eye.

Maybe I grew up far too quickly, or at least that's how it
looks.
That's a mystery of life to me. Like the day I was born, I don't
remember.

I don't remember when I crossed that line.
From innocent to callow youth.

From boy, to bold young rebel, to a man of many faces.
Maybe it was the first cigarette I smoked or the first beer at
New Year.
Grown up pursuits became much more desirable than
kicking a ball in the back courts.

It's the things I do remember that make me who and what I
really am. The scars, the warts and all, the roller coaster of
ambitious youth.

I will not die an unlived life.
I will not die without a try.
I will not dodge or evade the scrum.
I will not die before the outcome.
I will not die before the end, before the final curtain falls.

Street Life

Street life continued and boys will be boys! So it was for me on the streets of Glasgow in the 1950's and 1960's. We had moved to 27 Watt Street about 1967, a house with an inside toilet!
By this time I had developed a liking for flying homing pigeons, or "doos", as I called them. I had a wee Doo cat out of my bedroom window and would spend hours watching the birds coming and going.

Big John bought me my first two birds, Baldy and Big Dan. We went to a man in Dumbarton to get them, the first time I let them go, they promptly returned there!

I joined a wee pigeon club up at Scotland Street and started buying and selling birds. It was great fun and I met a few Glasgow characters who shared the same interest as me.
Every weekend we would fly our "doos" out of the window and try to catch birds belonging to other people. It was great fun and such a simple pastime. During the light nights we could be outside until all hours of the day just watching our pigeons flying back and forth.

Day trip to Edinburgh, Martha me and doos

I would be up to allsorts of mischief with my pals although, by and large, I managed to avoid the slashers and knife culture of the street gangs in Glasgow. It was more harmless pursuits such as climbing dykes in the back court or hitching rides, "hudgies" as we called them, on the back of moving buses and lorries. Real Artful Dodger stuff!

In the days before containerisation, all manner of goods would simply be transported on the backs of open lorries to the nearby docks. I hitched a ride on the lorries and along the way, helped myself to all manner of goodies. Everything from confectionery to beer or cider if you were lucky could be got from the moving vehicle. You waited until it stopped or slowed down at a corner, grabbed a handful and ran through the back courts clutching your bounty.

Sound familiar? Yes, this piracy seemed to run in the family! Just like my two Uncles of years gone by, I too eventually became unstuck!

One day on the way home from school, a few of us boys, being adept climbers, made our way over the gates of Hendry's lemonade factory. We were in heaven! We got tore into the bottles of juice and were very happy wee urchins indeed.

I, however, was later caught for my crime of drinking lemonade without the owner's permission.

As a 10 year old, I well remember the run up to my first court appearance as the worst feeling of my short life. Little knowing there was worse to come.

My Dad, big John, took me to court and stood beside me as the charges were read out. Theft of typewriters, a cash box and all manners of office equipment! I was charged with stealing the lot and was well and truly stitched up. I would have needed a van to transport everything I was accused of and me a wee boy of 10 years old. I was well fitted up for insurance purposes-common practice at the time.

I was asked how I was pleading and told by my Dad to plead guilty, even though I only took the lemonade. My Dad thought I would be treated leniently as it was my first offence.

No such luck for me. I was sentenced to 14 days in Larchgrove Remand Centre.

My mother was broken hearted, as well as my Dad, and I left for my punishment with my Sister's cries ringing in my ears.

I arrived at my new home as a relative "innocent in a foreign land". Sleeping accommodation was in dormitories housing 8-10 boys aged from 10-16 years old. Some of the boys were of shaving age and would often boast of their exploits. The oldest boy, Andy, would brag about stealing an old Austin car along with his friend and taking two girls out to the remote Fenwick Moor. On arriving at a suitable spot in the middle of nowhere they would turn to the girls and say "right girls, its cock it or walk it". I grew up pretty quickly in this environment.

Andy turned his attention to me saying "it's your first night and you're just in".

Pointing to the ceiling he said "See the green light and the red light up there? When the red light comes on, it's your turn to go to the square and get the cocoa and biscuits".

He was referring to the assembly area outside.

So. When the red light came on that night; I duly went to the deserted square and waited for someone to come with the cocoa and biscuits.

Well I waited and waited and waited. There was no sign of anyone and no cocoa or biscuits either. After a fair length of time, a supervisor approached and asked "what the hell are you doing out here?

I duly replied "the red light came on and I'm waiting for cocoa and biscuits sir".

He gave me a light cuff and pushing me gently said "get back to your f…ing dorm".

I quickly ran back indoors to discover that the lights were off and all the boys were in bed laughing at their initiation prank.

I later discovered that the red light meant no one was to leave the dorm as it would shortly be lights out for the night. Never mind the cocoa and biscuits!

I cried that night when the other boys were asleep, not from feeling homesick but from the humiliation of the initiation ceremony. It was only to get worse.

Round two came the following night when big Andy approached and asked to see my hand. He measured the width with his thumb and middle finger and looking towards his crotch said "yes that's just about the right size Iain".

Well, the implications of this led to another sleepless, fearful night for me.

The following day whilst I was in the toilet, Andy's "message boy" appeared on the scene. He explained that "tonight's the night for you boy as far as Andy is concerned".

This was my first violent outburst. I grabbed the boy by the ears and smashed his head off the wall. He screamed like a stuck pig and the supervisors came running in to the toilet.

The victim was given first aid and I was given six lashes with a belt on each hand by the boss man.

At least it was better than being big Andy's w….r and I was left alone after that episode. I was regarded as being a "headcase" and best avoided.

A week later my parents came to visit and it was the first and last time I saw my Dad crying. He couldn't speak to me and paced up and down, leaving Mum to ask me how I was being treated.

My Dad blamed himself for my situation. With the gift of hindsight it was rather like the guy in the Johnny Cash song "A boy named Sue" who had to get tough or die.

In my case, I had to toughen up to survive the detention.

When I returned home, Martha was delighted to be reunited with her brother again. It was not long, however, before the lesson wore off, and I was back into mischief once more!

Life goes on as the saying goes and it went on for me!

We stayed one time with Auntie Mary Frizell in Queensland Drive in Cardonald. Our Mum and Dad had gone to Uist for Uncle Angus's wedding and we were left with our cousins.

Johnnie Frizell and I were the same age and great pals; we later went out to Kuwait to work at the scaffolding and laying pipelines with my Dad.

We boys liked nothing better than to go along the railway line in Cardonald, oblivious to danger, and run across the line as a train was approaching. Daft wee boys playing daft games!

How we survived those days were a mystery to me then and now.

I had a great childhood with my cousins and we got up to all sorts of antics, both in Glasgow and up in Uist.

Johnnie's older Sister Patsy went on to become a nun and she also came with us one year to Uist. We were lucky to have such a large family and share good times. Our childhood was blessed and we were better off than a lot of other kids growing up in Glasgow.

Iain chasing Uncle Angus James and the tractor.

Uist Times

South Uist is a small island in the Outer Hebrides off the West Coast of Scotland. It is the place I regard as my spiritual home and the place where I have the happiest memories.

The island is made up of beautiful, white sandy beaches in the west and mountains in the east.
The centre is low lying and dotted with numerous small lochs.
Every summer, when school was over, we left the dirty city streets and headed north for our Summer Holidays. The journey commenced at Glasgow's Queen Street Station when we boarded the steam train bound for Oban. What a fantastic trip it was. Through Glencoe and Fort William and some of Scotland's finest scenery.
We would picnic on the train from flasks of tea and sandwiches before finally arriving in Oban for the next stage of our adventure. The Lochmor ferry, replaced by the Claymore, was a fantastic adventure playground for Martha and I. We ran wild on the ferry until it docked in Lochboisdale, usually around midnight. Our lovely Uncle Angus James would meet us with his ramshackle van to take us to Gran's house in Garrynamonie. I am sure the islanders thought they were being invaded by Glasgow hooligans every summer.

I remember one particular summer when my Mum's Sisters were all in Uist, with their families, at the same time.
Aunt Agnes had 6 children. The Perry family.
Aunt Morag had 7 children. The MacNeil family.
Aunt Katie Ann had 7 children. The McRury family.
Uncle Angus had 4 children. The MacDonald family.
My Mum had 2 children. The McColl family.
Do the maths and imagine my Grandmother watching that lot of an evening!

We were all in the one room with a double bed, cots and mattresses on the floor, complete with the "chanty" under the big bed.

At night we would lie in bed with the window open, listening to the Corncrakes in the field. It was still light at midnight and we were in no hurry to go to sleep!

One evening my Grandmother was watching the children as all the adults had gone off to a ceilidh. It was not long before we got up to mischief. The kids in the big double bed started using it as a trampoline. Granny was not amused! She was downstairs knitting and the ceiling was bouncing up and down due to yours truly jumping on the bed. The springs burst out of the old mattress and one pierced Martha in the leg. Well, Martha is hopping about with blood flowing freely down her leg and Granny opened the bedroom door. She spotted Martha out of bed and walloped her with a slipper! By this time I was back under the covers pretending to be asleep. Granny shouted at Martha to stop her carry on and get back into bed. Martha was trying to explain what had happened but Granny was having none of it!

My poor Sis had to go outside, find a docken leaf and administer first aid to herself. She wiped the wound clean with the leaf and returned to bed. Martha was always the sensible one in the family and I think she was given a double dose of common sense while I had none. Ah well. Brothers and Sisters will always carry on when their parents are out for the evening.

During the long summer days, Martha and I would get up to our shenanigans again.

One day we left the croft to saunter down to the beach, about a half mile down the road. We loved the "Machair" and often gathered limpets off the rocks, putting them in an old piece of sack and taking them home for boiling up for the dinner along with lovely Uist potatoes. It was a simple meal but would fill you up after a hard day getting into mischief!

We stopped at the house of Donald Hector Mc Neil, a close friend of Uncle Angus and author of the play which Mum had a wee role in.

There were a few of his chickens around, clucking and pecking away. Well Martha and I decided they were in need of a wee shampoo and looked around the byre for some suitable liquid with which to carry out the job. We discovered a drum of old tractor oil, which we poured along the centre trough in the byre designed to accommodate the flow of dung from the cattle stalls. We sprinkled chicken feed on the oil to entice the birds and bingo! The chickens received their "shampoo and set" but some ate the oil covered maize feed and promptly died later that day.

Well, after this little mischievous interlude we carried on to the beach and paddled in the Atlantic Ocean for a wee while before returning home for dinner.

News travels fast on an island and we had a welcoming committee at Gran's front door when we got home. Mum, Gran, Aunt Agnes and Granddad were not amused by our antics, never mind Donald Hector, the owner of the chickens.
Mum was armed with a rubber hosepipe, which was used to fill up the old Hoover twin tub washing machine and she gave us quite a thrashing with it. We were belted on our backsides and soon came out in big welts caused by the beating we received. Granddad was sitting on an old wooden bench smoking his pipe of black twist tobacco and decided enough was enough.

"Leave him alone Annie" he said. "He will be a good man some day".

I wish to God his prediction had been right. Granddad. My Saviour.

What you have to remember is there was no Child Line in those days or Chicken Line either!

Mum obviously regarded our antics as very serious as that was the only time I remember her lifting her hand to us with such severity.

Life in Uist continued at a slow pace and days were filled with chores. Lifting peat and haymaking were hard physical tasks for young children but we never complained. We did have plenty time for enjoying ourselves too.

One hot summer day, Martha and I were playing at the side of the road outside the croft house. There was a wee burn, which trickled right down the roadside through the village and we had an old tea strainer with us. We were trying to catch some eels when along the road we spotted a neighbour walking. Willie Mc Kenzie was a giant of a man at well over 6ft in height. He was carrying a shepherd's crook and had his collie dog with him. He was going over the hill from Garrynamonie to Glendale to look for some lost sheep. We asked if we could accompany him on his search and he agreed, providing we had permission from Mum. I think I was around 6 years old then and Mum reluctantly gave permission for us to go. She had some misgivings that we would run out of stamina before we climbed the hill!

Off we set through Garrynamonie, with Willie leading the way like the Pied Piper and Martha bringing up the rear with the dog. I was allowed to carry the crook, which was over 6 feet long and I was proud as punch! By the time we arrived at the peat bogs at the bottom of the hill, Martha and I were squabbling again! I started chasing her through the bogs, waving the stick at her, and she slipped into one of the soft peat bogs. It was about 12 inches deep and she got stuck fast in the black, peaty soil. She was squealing like a stuck pig before Willie came to the rescue and fished her out with his crook. What a sight she was, totally covered in black soil up to her knees and her wellies getting sooked off her legs. We pulled the wellies off and dipped her in a river to wash the muck off then rinsed out her wellies! She was quite the wee trooper though and soon squished her feet back into the soggy boots. It must have been very uncomfortable for her to walk in them as later on that night, when we got back home, her feet and legs were red raw and Mum smothered them with baking soda to try and cool them down!

Not to be put off, we continued our climb and eventually reached the top. Willie stopped for a breather and we admired the view while he pointed out the various islands around us. We got a wee drink of peaty water from a stream and carried on down to South Glendale in our quest to find the missing sheep. They were eventually located on a small island but luckily the tide was out and the dog was dispatched to round them up. All we needed was a couple of horses and it would be like being in a film. A Western with sheep instead of cattle!

Next step was the return journey and boy, were we tired out. We started dragging our heels back to the top of the hill and it was not too long before we had to stop for a wee breather. By this time we had been out for 5 hours with no food and our wee legs had had enough for one day. There was no bus to take us home and it was at least another 2 hour walk before we got off the hill. Martha was hoisted on to Willie's shoulders but I refused the offer to take his hand. I was a big man, after all and I had my pride! It was not long before I lagged further and further behind and all I could hear was Martha saying to Willie
"Just leave him; he can get home on his own".
So much for Sisterly loyalty! We did eventually make it back home and sat down with Willie and his wife, to a feast fit for a king. After scoffing 3 boiled eggs each, scones and a cup of tea

we headed back to our Gran's house for a well earned rest. I decided that day that I would never be a shepherd as it was all too much like hard work.

Uncle Angus had an old shotgun and I was dying to try it out shooting rabbits on the beach. One evening the men folk in the house set off on a hunting trip. Dad, Uncle Bill Perry, Uncle Angus and I all toddled down to see what we could shoot on the shore. As we passed big Willie Mc Kenzie's house he stood watching us approaching. He commented that we looked like Dad's Army and said he would lock up the sheep in case we missed our target! We carried on and soon we were lying on our bellies in the grass waiting for rabbits to appear. I begged to have the first shot and the adults agreed, despite promising Mum they would not let me shoot the gun.

Unknown to us, the gun had not been cleaned or fired for a number of years, so when I took careful aim at Bugs Bunny, holding the gun John Wayne style, and the gun backfired on me. I got thrown on to my back and had a bruised cheek and shoulder. We had to tell Mum that I tripped and fell on a stone. I, however, suspect that she did not believe a single word!

On another occasion I went out sea fishing, in the Sound of Eriskay, with a friend of Dad's. We took the gun along in case we spotted any low flying ducks we could shoot and have for dinner. Alas, the same thing happened when I fired the gun and I was thrown backwards in the boat. Cue another bruised cheek and I decided that shooting was maybe not for me after all!

I remember the first time I saw my Uncle Angus killing a sheep. He took it in the barn and locked the sheep's head between his knees. Taking his knife, which he normally used for cutting his black twist tobacco, he slit the throat and hung the sheep on a hook. My Sister, Martha, grabbed a bucket to catch the blood which was used to make black pudding. The chops and mutton, my mother took back to Glasgow to feed the family. We gathered some new potatoes from the shore and we dined like royalty on our return to Glasgow! We thought nothing of killing animals for food and many a time my Grandmother would send me to catch a chicken. She showed me how to wring its neck quickly and how to pluck the feathers. It would then be singed over an open fire before being boiled for soup and eating the meat afterwards. There was never any food wasted on the croft.

As I grew into my teens, I left school at the age of 15, without a qualification of any kind, and went to my first job working at a company called P and F Hecht in Oswald St, Glasgow. I was the "gofer" and one of my chores was to get the rolls and sandwiches for the staff at lunchtime. The two bosses were of the Jewish faith and being a bit of a comedian, I would constantly joke about rolls with ham or rolls with pork!

Needless to say, the job and I parted company.

I, however, had another string to my bow and achieved my ambition to go and work in South Uist alongside Uncle Angus. My father thought this would shake up my ideas and turn me into a man!
We worked on the shore gathering the seaweed, or tangle, and taking it along to the seaweed factory at Daliburgh. It was then dried out and processed before being sent off in powder form. It has many uses including: cosmetics, pet food, and a gelling agent in ice cream and noodles! Who would have thought it?

The job was hard work but well paid. I sent money home to Mum and gave some to Aunt Mary for my keep. I always wanted to build a house on Uist in the field in Garrynamonie pointed out to me by Uncle Angus. Uist will always be my spiritual home. It is where I feel most at peace with myself and Martha knows my final wish in regard to Uist.

I was referred to affectionately as "The Lowlander's son". With all this excess cash in my pocket and nothing to do on the island, I turned to whisky.

I did damage to myself and I paid the price. It took many years of struggling to beat the demon drink but I did it my way! Drink and drugs played a large part in my downfall and contributed to my ill health. I have many regrets but no one else was to blame for my antics.

As a teenager on Uist I would ride my 5 speed gear bike for miles along the single track roads. I would call in at houses and get fed all over the island. Boiled eggs and home made scones were a favourite of mine. Sometimes I would get out for a days fishing with an islander and in return for helping out, I would bring home herring or mackerel for the dinner.

I would often visit the O' Henley family living in the next croft. What great times I had with Wee Angus, Big Angus, Roddy and Donald Alastair. We would share a wee dram and talk nonsense, swapping stories of times gone by. They were like surrogate fathers to me those men and I grew very fond of them as well as enjoying their company.

Sometimes, in the evening, I would go and play cribbage and poker with my Uncle Ewen Steele who lived in a wee thatched cottage a short distance away. There was no electricity or running water but it was very cosy. Light was supplied from Tilly lamps filled with paraffin, I think, or from candles and the water came from a nearby well. He would send me off on my bike to the pub for a half bottle of whisky and, on my return, tell me stories of his life as a young man while he taught me how to play a mean game of poker. What a fascinating character he was. He had worked in Canada during his youth, logging on the Great Lakes. Whilst at work one day jumping from log to log, he slipped and fell, sustaining an injury to his leg. He always walked with a limp after that, a permanent reminder of his time working at the logging.

I never found out if the story about the limp was true…but it was a good story!!

The wee house is no longer there and it is sad when I go past the site as I have so many happy memories of my time spent there. We stayed there one year when Gran's house was full of people.

It was a cosy wee thatched house full of memories. I would love to see a house built there but it is an unfulfilled dream.

Polachar Inn on South Uist, where Iain would visit for his Uncle Ewen. Iain spent many an evening there when he worked on Uist.

Garrynamonie Machair on South Uist
This is where Iain worked for some time gathering seaweed.
Probably his favourite place on earth.

Back in Glasgow

All good things must come to an end and so, after a year on Uist, albeit reluctantly, I returned home.

I had gone from boy to man in a year and acquired many bad habits!

My next employment was in a local factory manufacturing dog food. I was bored stupid but the pay was good.

Every Friday evening the employees received the bashed tins of dog food to give to their own pets.

I, however, had other money making ideas and went round the local shops selling cases of dog food at cheap prices. My Dad, who by this time, had a shop in Elder Street in Govan, would take some and sell them at reduced prices.

Martha and I would go into the shop on Sundays and give Dad some time off.

I remember one particular day a young lad, who stayed in Garmouth St, came into the shop brandishing a piece of wood. I was in the back shop relaxing and letting Martha do all the hard work, as usual. I heard her shouting "f..k you" and ran to see what the commotion was.

Martha had a big cheese knife in her hand waving it at the ambitious robber but he quickly bolted and ran off home.

We reported the incident to our Dad and the following day he took me to the house where the lad lived. His Mum was a good customer and Dad would often give her "tick" or credit.

We knocked the door and Dad explained to the mother just what had happened in the shop the previous day. The woman was affronted and called her son to the door. She grabbed him by the scruff of the neck and threw him into the close. "Take your punishment like a man" she said.

We went into the back court and slugged it out, with me emerging as the winner.

Justice was done and we never had any more trouble after that.

My Grandmother McColl, another Martha, also had a wee shop in Golspie St. She would regularly send me to the cash and carry on Shaw St for cigarettes to sell in the shop.

I was returning from my errand one day, carrying a holdall full of cigarettes, when I was pounced on by 3 toe rags trying to rob me.

I hung on for grim death and bolted back to the shop.

My Grandfather,"Fogarty" as we called him affectionately, was in the shop. We wandered back down Golspie St to look for the 3 musketeers and spied them in the phone box outside the Boars Head pub. Well, Fogarty held the door closed and one by one dragged the boys out of the phone kiosk for me to administer justice. In those days you dished out your own revenge and that was it sorted. Survival of the fittest!

My Aunt Mary Frizell also delivered swift retribution to a young man who tried to rob my wee Granny.

The young thug tried to hold up the shop and Mary lifted the heavy padlock and walloped him round the side of his head!

The local beat bobby was in the following day and commented that a certain local celebrity was sporting a rather sore head!

In 1970, my wee brother Donny was born. I was 16 then and Martha was 15.

Every Saturday, Mum would go to the shop to help Dad with the chores and Martha would babysit Donny. In the afternoon I would settle in to watch wrestling on television, Big Daddy and Mick Mc Manus were my favourites. Martha would make us a Vesta boil in the bag curry! Simple pleasure indeed and this led to me having a lifetime love of spicy food.

Granny McColl's shop at 86 Golspie Street and the scene of Govan style justice. The telephone kiosk at the Boars head! Fogarty and Iain were a formidable team.

The power cuts of 1971-1972 provided us with a veritable Klondike in the shop. We had a source for candles, namely a local woman who worked in the candle factory in Govan. She would fill her car boot with cases of them and deliver them to the shop in Elder Street. Everyone was sold out of candles, due to being left in darkness at night, except us!

Word soon got out that big John had a supply of candles and without being too greedy, we still made a tidy wee profit.

Some customers came just to buy a candle but many became customers for life after this.

My Dad often gave credit to women who were struggling to buy food for their children and indeed, I remember him having unpaid credit at the end of the week but never once did he push anyone for payment.

He was a very generous man was John and never forgot his roots. I remember being taken along the River Clyde where many homeless people would sit. Dad often brought cigarettes and distributed them to the homeless. Sometimes he would send me along to the fish and chip shop on Paisley Rd and I would return with bags of hot chips for men less fortunate than myself.

John would often say "Never judge anyone son. You never know what lies ahead of you".

I never forgot my father's words. Little did I know then of the hardships ahead of me and the road I would travel.

As time marched on and I found myself without work, I dabbled in a wee bit of song writing. My cousin Donny MacNeil, Drummer with the Vatersay Boys, was also doing a wee bit of writing.

We composed a wee song called **"The Giro Song"** sung to the tune of "Blanket on the Ground".

I would sing this ditty when I was standing in the queue at the Job Centre (or Buroo) in Pollokshaws.

The Giro Song

I must get up at 9 this morning
There's a task I have to do
I've got to go down by the river
Cos its today I sign the buroo
Just because I'm not working don't mean I can't have a ball
With my giro in my pocket I'll get drunk and spend it all

I remember when I was working with my shoulder to the wheel.
For the coppers I was earning, you know it truly wasn't real.
I decided I would chuck it, have it all on a plate.
I go down and join the scroungers,
We can all live off the state,

Just because I'm not working don't mean I can't have a ball
With my giro in my pocket I'll get drunk and spend it all.

And I wake up the next morning and I'll be skint once again
Never mind it won't be long till my next buroo day
When I sign at half past 10.
Just because I'm not working don't mean I can't have a ball
With my giro in my pocket I'll get drunk and spend it all.

Now, one day I decided I had had enough of signing on, and Donnie and I were standing in the queue of unemployed men. A pretty long queue it was too!

When my turn arrived, I asked the poor woman behind the desk if I could take all my papers and sign off. She duly refused and we started singing the Giro Song. The place was in an uproar and we were asked to leave by the staff. We left to the tune ringing in our ears as the other men in the queue were repeating the chorus!

By this stage of my life, the shop in Govan closed and I went out to Kuwait with my Dad to work at installing the oil pipelines in the desert. What a fortune we made out there. My cousin Johnnie Frizell also came out to work and we had some great times in the desert. It was hard work but well paid. Alas, all good things have to end and when the contract finished, Dad and I returned home to Glasgow.

Iain & Dad in Kuwait

My thoughts then turned to acting. It was a natural progression for me as I was forever playing the fool! My friend Joe Greenan was always encouraging me to give it a go. He said I was a natural!

I attended an audition at the old RSAMD in Buchanan Street in Glasgow and, much to my amazement; I was accepted on to the course. It was great fun acting the fool and a proud day for my family, when I graduated with the Gold Medal for Comedy, presented to me by the late great Iain Cuthbertson. My Mum and Sister attended the graduation.

Dad never showed much emotion and thought his rebel son was a bit too big for his boots! He thought if he could pull in the reins a bit, his rebel son might just turn out fine!

Iain and Martha at his graduation.

After graduating, I landed a role in Bill Forsyth's "Comfort and Joy". I played the part of a big, scary, Glaswegian character who went around beating up ice cream vans.

It was great fun to do and I learned a lot about acting. Bill Paterson was the star, with Alex Norton also appearing and Ross King, who was a DJ on Clyde, starred as an extra.

That December, 1983, my father died suddenly at 53 years of age. I struggled to cope with his death and have done all my life. My brother in law, Frank Gibbons, came out to Motherwell to tell me the sad news. He was a Police officer but I know he found it difficult to relate the details of what had happened. He had tears in his eyes as he told me that "Big John" had suffered a fatal heart attack at his work and he had died instantly.

I was doing panto there at the time, Babes in the Wood.
Phil Mc Call was the Dame and I was Big Ben. Tony Roper was also appearing in the panto.
I don't know where I found the strength to carry on with the performance that night but Phil and Tony were a great support. The show must go on after all and you can't let people down.
The saying "tears of a clown" was very true that day.
I have regrets that my Dad never saw me perform on stage or in films or television. I like to think that, in his own way, he was proud of his big son for the way he turned out.

Not long after this, I met Nora Friel and we were married in Glasgow. We moved over to Argyll, near Kilfinan. It was a ramshackle of a house with a couple of acres. We had Bob, the Welsh Mountain pony and Squash, the Cairn terrier dog as well as our 3 children, Rhianan, Ciaran and Maurice. There was a mud track about a mile long that you had to walk up to get to the house. Nice and remote and peaceful for a troubled actor like me! **I loved the solitude of the area and it reminded me of Uist.**

Of all the good things I ever did in life, my children were the best.

My life then spiralled quickly downhill.
I was not the greatest husband or father and I was drinking heavily. I did damage and I paid the price. I have regrets and pain and put my hands up to my downfall.

Too many nights spent in the Downfall Bar.

The alcohol, drugs and anti-depressants took a toll on my life, family and career. I felt my life spiralling away from me and it felt like I was on a rollercoaster that never stopped. I was a wild one, a hell raiser and a drunk. I blew it big time. I could have been a millionaire and a big star. Nobody to blame but myself.

I often sought sanctuary in Nunraw Abbey, outside Edinburgh. It was a chance to get away from the pressures of life and my addiction to alcohol and other substances. The solitude gave me time to reflect on my life and I rediscovered my faith. My religion brought me comfort throughout my illness and helped me to find an inner peace. I was never afraid of death, only of the demons in my head.

SAINT IAIN? – "AYE RIGHT."

Bipolar Bro
Thoughts from brother Donnie

The earliest and fondest memory I have of my big brother was when he bought my first bike, a Raleigh Drifter BMX type if my memory is right, with drum rear brake, delivered in the Buckshot van him Mick and Donny our cousins used to move their music gear round in, it was a great bike. Iain's heart was in the right place but he was a wild untameable man also and at times unbearable and impossible to live with. Iain used to tell me of days with our cousins and the band and their optics in the back of the van, hard rockers.

I used to pick up a local hard guy in Nitshill when out in my minicab, when he heard Iain was my brother he told me about a time years ago in the Royal Oak pub, Iain made everyone laugh so much that he was taken hostage to someone's house and fed booze and drugs for 3 days to keep the guys entertained.

Iain once sent me a postcard when I was in Primary School from when he was holidaying in Greece with Joe Greenan; a lovely man, great musician and family friend (Iain called Joe his brother from another mother), the card just said:

"Weathers here, wish you were Lovely".

Iain always dreamt of building a house for all the family in South Uist where our Mum grew up, on a wee plot he said our Uncle Angus James promised to him, nothing written though, just a verbal promise. He never realised that dream and I wish I could have helped him with that.

Iain married Nora soon after our Dad passed away in 1984 and they had their 3 kids soon after that. Rhianan, Ciaren and Maurice didn't always have it easy growing up....

Iain asked if he could park a small caravan for a while in our driveway, I declined knowing that my wife Tracy would not be amused to say the least. A couple of days later a car comes in the street with a caravan in tow and before I could get my shoes on Iain was guiding the driver into our driveway. As I'm working out what just happened off the driver went and we now have a caravan in the drive! Needless to say when Tracy got home the shit really hit the fan.

She agreed it could stay for a few days, which came and went. Then, when she rang Iain to arrange its departure, he gave her short shrift and said he would move it when he was good and ready. Tracy called Iain again to find out where he was and went to have it out with him. No small task but she is well able to hold her own. As he was pretty well cheeky to her about the whole thing she told him to move it within an hour or she would phone a scrap yard to take it for free.

Within an hour or so it was gone, much to the dismay of my son Ciaren who wanted to sleep in it overnight with his pals, nae joy sunshine.

In the summer of 2012 I asked Iain if he would like our garden shed as we wanted to get rid of it, (it used to be our Mums so had lots of sentimental value) but I didn't want to bin it so thought he could use it for "fleein the doos". He agreed, so I took it apart and told him to get a van to move it.

Weeks went past then there was a stormy few days during which our back garden fence blew over, along with the shed panels which were stacked against it. Still no sign of Iain with the van.

One Sunday afternoon out of the blue Iain appears with his pal John Sanderman in a Vauxhall Astra estate.
Iain came into the house in a hell of a mood and starts to engage me in an all out argument for no apparent reason! Then he storms out the back garden and drags the shed out to the car and tries to put the panels on the roof, which had NO roof-rack, scraping all the paintwork on John's car during the process. All the while ranting away like a crazy person. So he says "F..k it I'll phone a taxi to take it." Just bully for me who has one parked outside the house.

My 6 year old son Calum even confronted him and says,

"Uncle Iain you won't fit the shed in a taxi".

Iain stood there looking down at this wee boy like a raging bull but didn't say a word to the wee one. If it was an adult, he looked like he would have tore him to shreds, a truly surreal moment, which wouldn't have been believed if not seen by all involved, which by chance included Iain's son Maurice and his girlfriend Emma, who had coincidentally appeared for a visit.

This was the first time I encountered Iain's Bipolar first hand. My wife Tracy during the whole episode recognised right away that this wasn't Iain's normal behaviour and it turned out he hadn't been taking his meds.

At my next birthday Iain gave me a card saying
"Happy Birthday from your Bipolar Bro."

We had a laugh at that although poor John's car was never the same again! He also gave Calum, who had been through an operation in one eye, a Bible which was stuffed with Iraqi Dinar. We can only speculate the origins of the cash, I would try and exchanged the Dinar but only Iain knew were it came from.

Many a Christmas Iain spent with us, he was such a laugh when he was on form and he was usually on good form. Tracy's Mum and Gran would have a right giggle over Christmas dinner, he was ever the entertainer. I sometimes wondered if it was a trait of entertainers and if they were all like Iain with his split personality.

The Dunoon ferry.

My Sister Martha bought me my first car, a 1.3 Mk II Ford Escort, sought after cars when I was 17 but it was a bucket of crap and leaked like a sieve. (Sorry Sis) I loved that car as it had a great engine. It took Iain, Nora, the kids and me many times over the mountains to their house, "Acharossan," in Argyll when their kids were small. The kids used to love those journeys; we would pack sandwiches a flask of tea and treats for the wee ones for stopping on the way in the mountains of Argyll.

Iain asked me to drive him home from Glasgow to Acharossan one day which I was more than pleased to do and off we went, Nora, my Sister in law was, at home with the kids. Not thinking much of it I got to the start of the dirt track which led a mile and half to the house only to notice I was out of fuel. I asked Iain if he could spot me a twenty to get home, some 75 miles away, to which he said "I don't have any money", and buggered off on his walk up the track!

I had 2 options

1) Drive over the "Rest and Be Thankful," through Arrochar and definitely run out of fuel on the way.
2) Nurse the car over the hills to Dunoon and work it out from the Ferry Terminal and hope I would make it.

I opted for number 2, made it to Dunoon and went to the local Police Station to ask if they could help and I would pay them back at Pollok Police Office when I got home. Heaven knows what they thought but they gave me cash for a ferry ticket and fuel when I thought they would have told me to get lost!

Iain at times was difficult to live with.
Nora used to always say
"Would the real Iain McColl please stand up?"

The Green Car

Iain never had any luck with green cars.

He once owned a vintage Rolls Royce Bentley, a beautiful old car. It was silver with a 4 Litre V8 engine and column shift gears. It took 4 adults and 4 kids on a trip to Donegal faithfully with no problems. When Iain was selling it, while reversing it out of the driveway he clipped a street pole, tore off the front bumper and made quite a dent. Iain was livid and on closer scrutiny it seemed the car had been re-sprayed - originally it had been green. Needless to say that made his fury a whole lot worse.

Tighnabruaich

When Iain and Nora bought Acharossan they had an old pickup truck for moving furniture and things up to the house, a green one as it happens. On the way there one night going through Greenock heading to the ferry we stopped at a petrol station and pulled in beside a couple of traffic cops who proceeded to look over the van.

Springs were sticking through the floor so it was impounded, but Iain was "pounded" too for drunk driving, unbeknown to me, there were 2 shotguns under the seats which Iain had procured to do a spot of shooting in Argyll. Knowing Iain we can only speculate as to what he was going to be shooting!
Iain went to court in Dunoon for that and was sent to Jail. It was not Iain's first or last encounter with the law or prison.

Iain was often difficult to live with but I am and always was proud of him, he really was better at his job than he was given credit for, few in the profession acknowledged it as he was a bit of a wildcard. Martin Scorsese gave him great plaudits during filming of Gangs of New York in Rome.

He graduated from The Royal Scottish Academy of Music and Drama with two gold medals which, to date, only Iain has achieved in Scotland; he won Best Actor and Best Comedy Actor. We recently visited the new Hard Rock Café in Glasgow and dined where the stage used to be, you can still hear the "Clockwork Orange" (Glasgow Underground Railway) rumble by. They put on some great shows and Iain graduated there.

He did lots of Panto over the years which he really enjoyed and some of his TV moments are memorable, he usually played a dim witted character but was far cleverer than portrayed in his roles. He admired Ricky Fulton, Jack Milroy, Stanley Baxter, Chic Murray and other Scots comedians of old and he impersonated Tommy Cooper very well in a one man tour round the country, it was quite a success.

He got the family involved doing "extra work" which I always enjoyed. Mum especially enjoyed it; she is on screen in some films which is great. Being in the "Green Room," during filming of City Lights at age 16 was quite something. Growing up with an actor brother and rock star cousins (Mick MacNeil was at the height of his career with Simple Minds at the time) was odd. To everyone its like, "wow Big Tam is your brother," but he wasn't Big Tam he was just my big bro Iain. So I don't really ever look at celebrities with Star Struck eyes.

Iain got me 2 weeks work on the movie "Stroke of Genius" about the golfer Bobby Jones. Filming was in St Andrews, on the old golf courses. My job was driving cast, crew and extras around the town to and from locations. Working in TV and film is great, well paid, and you get well fed but the hours are very long. However, the folk you can bump into are fantastic and I met some really nice people over the years.

It is well documented in the media about Iain's wild side. From the outside you may think it's great to have celebrity and great for the family, but its not all smiles and roses, especially in the Goldfish bowl that is Glasgow. Almost every time Iain put a foot wrong it was in the news papers, mostly one in particular.

This had a profound effect on me and the family from very early on in his acting career. Later on it hurt even more when I saw the damage it was causing his children from their teens into twenties but it was worsened tenfold when it ended up that often Iain was the one giving the story in the first place!

I heard it said that he got too famous, too quick. I used to urge him to leave Glasgow altogether and go to London but he never did. He shouldn't have had to but the media were too claustrophobic for him. He banjoed at least one reporter in his time due to the pressure they put him under.

In some ways Iain is immortalised as we can always shove a DVD in the machine to see and hear him again. I consider myself lucky that I can do that as most people can't. It was, and is hard to lose a brother but now I always remember him with a laugh, even when Iain was at his lowest during chemotherapy he still had folk laughing.

This book will acknowledge all at the Beatson but I am personally very grateful to Dr Soutar who did all he could for Iain, all the staff that put up with so much from Iain and all at "Friends of The Beatson," a great resource.

The condemned man in Gangs of New York
Martin Scorsese described Iain as "A great method actor".

Mick MacNeil

It was early summer, sometime in the late nineties. I was mostly sleeping on the drum room floor of my basement studio, Iain called in often, we would either set up a mic, maybe record an old Alex Harvey tune with some ad-lib ("we gave it Laldy, up in Darnley," I remember that lyric) - or just have a few beers with a joint. My marriage had been on the rocks for some time, I believe his was too.

"Let's do something" Iain said, I had read that there was a showing of "Braveheart" somewhere near Parkhead; it was a one off drive in movie experience. My fancy V12 Jag had been parked on Berkeley Street, in Glasgow with a flat tyre for about a month. Iain said
"Aye, are you in the AA? Let's get that fired up"
So we did, after the car was sorted, we then found out that the film was totally sold out.

Well we just had a few drinks more to think about plan B.

"Let's get a couple of birds, take them up the hills and shag them."
Said Iain. Now, that's the kind of idea I would have heard from a couple of 16 year old school boys, not two guys nearer 40, but at the time that was the best idea I'd heard in years. The studio was located next to a hostel so finding girls who wanted to have a look round Scotland was not a problem, we just needed at least one with a valid driving licence. We found a lovely American girl who was travelling round the world, Elizabeth, and my wee pal Lou who I was working with at the time. After getting stacked up with some Tequila and a tank full of petrol, we hit the road.

Iain was in the back with Lou, only because it was my car I felt obliged to co-pilot. Van Morrison songs all the way till, I think it was Aviemore, we decided to check into a hotel for the night, by this time I was well out of it. My only memory was of Iain making an agreement with Elizabeth that if they were both still single in exactly ten years from that day, they would marry each other!

When I woke for a late breakfast, no one was to be seen. I went for a stroll along the main street; I looked into a small gift shop and saw both Iain and Lou with sunglasses and hats on. The kind of hat you see the mother of the bride wear at a 1970's wedding. With an American accent Iain said "I am Clyde Barrow and this here is my partner, Bonnie Parker, and We Rob Banks" It seems they were going into all the shops to deliver this same line. The little woman serving didn't know what to make of it at all; she just had a baffled look on her face!

After we found Elizabeth and topped up our carry-oot, we loaded Van the Man or sometimes, the Lighthouse Family, "gona get lifted" to the CD and north we headed. Lou had some friends in Nairn that we decided to SURPRISE. It turned out that Lou's pals were quite a few in numbers, a kind of wee hippy community, so we settled in there quite the thing, passing the pipes of Peace and Love man.

Iain, wasn't the fastest on the draw at getting out the wallet, I had insisted that dinner tonight was his shout. "OK anyone up for Indian? It's on me" said Iain. We must have been at least a dozen in number and quite oiled by this time, so the restaurant owner put us in a private room kind of upstairs and round the back. He also allocated us our own waiter. At dinner Iain really was on form, he had us splitting our sides, with tears of laughter. "Another bottle of Hitlers Laughing Gear" he would announce. That's Liebfraumilch wine to you and me.

As soon as Iain paid the bill, he put a fiver at the end of the table as a tip for our waiter, giving the young man a wee wink. I remember thinking this bill must be at least £300 quid. A fiver wow! The owner came bouncing in carrying a large kitchen knife, waving it and shouting at Iain,

"I stab you, you bastard, I stab you, I stab you. You have chased all my customers away with all noise in here"

I have never seen Iain run from anybody. All the others silenced in a kind of "what's going." on numbness, but Iain walked straight over to him and said, slowly

"Go on then, stab me"

The mad Indian just kept bouncing and shouting, "I stab you I stab you."

Iain wasn't letting go, almost insisting that the nutter carry out his threats,

"Come on and stab me then."

The Police are now entering; the Indian must have called them before he started with the stab you stuff, the more senior looking one immediately goes to calm down the knife wielding nutter. It's clear they already knew each other. Anywhere else this guy would have been arrested already. While the younger cop tries to usher us out, Iain is having none of it. I don't know what it was with Iain and Police. Joey from Friends summed it up,

"Like a moth to the flame."

Iain was now insisting that this mad Indian carry out his threat and stab him.

"Between you me and The Sun." was a quote Iain often used, with the same quote I started to push Iain to the door. By now he was livid with anger, he could see the friendly chat going on between the Owner and the senior cop, as we passed the younger Policeman, Iain leaned forward, inches from his face, and whispered,

"That's right, take the side of the Hamilton Ackie."

The cop breathed out and went for his radio, I guess to call for a Van to jail us all. I pushed Iain towards the door, but first as he walked past the end of the table he casually picked up the tip, and said,

"You'll no be having that either."

Then legged it out the door.

Iain was due to go back to Glasgow for some kind of end of series screening thing at the BBC studios in Queen Margaret drive, In the back of my head, I only wanted to keep going north, things were getting more serious and I was thinking more of my kids and missing them, then I remembered, I'd heard about a place up here, that people go to get away from themselves, with no pubs. I felt the whole reason I'd had gone on this trip in the first place was to get to this place.

Findhorn is where I was looking for. So, in the middle of the night, Elizabeth and I did a runner and left Iain and Lou to sort themselves out. We ended up at Thurso, wondering if I could get a Ferry to take me north.

That didn't happen, so we started on the road back. Still playing Van the Man, now I was the only one drinking, and I was missing my pals, I told Elizabeth that it was really Lou that I wanted to be with, and could she take me to her. I fell asleep crying in the back seat

We all met up at the studio again the next day, and went off to the BBC with Iain to see the show he had been recording. And we were all pals again.

So a new plan: lets go to Chelsea. We decided to wait till morning, sort some stuff out then go for it in a oner. Setting off late, it was a long drive, the Tequila ran out about Birmingham and by the time we got to London it was too late for the off-licence. And I knew then, that I was a raging Alcoholic. Iain said "try AA, it worked for me for 3 years, but every man's his own mechanic".

Over the next few days, we just hung out on the Kings Rd, and when Iain left to go back to Glasgow, Lou and I stayed, and went to an AA meeting.

You could say the AA started and finished this story. I have never drank or taken drugs since. God Bless you Iain McColl. X

Yes, going over that story really was an emotional roller coaster journey that I feel both Iain and I shared. From extreme happiness to deep, deep sadness. I believe all funny people have this extreme emotion, Iain included, and it was my pleasure to go on that, last great road trip!

My cousin Michael did not have his sorrows to seek with Iain! I am very grateful to him for sharing his story publicly.

Bonnie and Clyde
The good old days on the road trip with Mick

Donny MacNeil, Iain and Mick MacNeil taken in the late 70's

John Quinn

(John designed the book cover)

I first met Iain McColl back in the 1980's when I worked as an art director making TV commercials in the ad agency business. I remember him as a Glaswegian street newspaper seller in a TV ad... I think it was for a bank... suffices to say, his performance was infinitely more memorable than the product, or brand, being promoted.... He was so outrageously funny.

Later on I got to know him really well after meeting him on a number of occasions at his cousin Mick MacNeil's recording studio in Berkeley Street.

Mick had already been a mate of mine for quite a few years and Iain and Mick were always up to some mischief with recording gear. Funny? Aye. Iain was one of the funniest, daftest guys you could ever meet. Most of the time he'd either have you in stitches laughing at something he'd done or said... or he'd be attempting some madcap stunt like trying to hypnotize you!

As time went by though, it became clear to me that underneath all the craziness there was a really decent, big guy who, at times, just like most of the rest of us, had his struggles in life and demons to fight.

I never fully appreciated how good an actor Iain really was until I saw his one-man performance as Tommy Cooper at the old Gaiety Theatre down in Ayr. The show was focused around Tommy's last night... when he really did die on stage. Iain was absolutely brilliant... Honestly, one of the best pieces of acting I've ever seen. I told him as much on numerous occasions and all I ever got back from him was "D'ye think so? ...Aye!... Cheers" accompanied by a huge grin.

Iain McColl... a great pal... fantastic fun... a total professional.

Jamie Doherty (a good friend of Iain)

When we lived in Pollok, our neighbour across the street was a guy called Jamie Doherty who later moved to Aberdeen. Iain and Jamie got on really well and were very fond of each other.

This is Jamie's memory of Iain.

When Iain was on tour with City Lights in Aberdeen, Iain's Mum, Annie, phoned me and asked if it would be ok for Iain to stay with Liz and I for the week, as he had been off the drink for nearly a year, and she didn't want him falling off the wagon. I told her it wouldn't be problem. Anyway, up he came and stayed with us. My friend had a business called Rainbow Glass; they fitted double glazed windows, he asked if I could get Iain to do a commercial on the local radio station (Northsound Radio). So Iain did one as Tommy Cooper, and we both did another with Iain as Dodie and me as Jamesy from Rab C. We got £100 each for our efforts. The guys in our studio, and those coming in from other studios to watch us were wetting themselves at our antics.

After the week Iain insisted on giving us £75 for letting him stay. I tried my best not to take it, but he wasn't having it. Anyway, after a couple of weeks, I got my phone bill in......he'd only been phoning a gambling premium hotline number and ran up £75 extra on my phone bill. I was blaming Graham, my son, as he was living with us at the time...Graham swore it wasn't him...so I rang the number on my detailed phone bill and that's how I found out it was a tipsters hotline!

There was another time, when, sitting in lounge in the Royal Oak pub in Nitshill, Iain walked in, put a cigarette in his mouth, pulled a Zippo lighter out from his pocket, ran the Zippo up a guys arm, up to his shoulder, lit the fag, and walked out. All this without speaking a word to anyone! The whole table was in stitches. I suppose if it hadn't worked, he would have sat down and joined us for a drink!

Then there was the time when Mick MacNeil and I went up to South Uist, when Iain worked in the Seaweed Factory in his teens. Mick took a bottle up for Angus James, Iain's Uncle, who went missing for 2 days! We hired pushbikes for the day then took the ferry to Barra without returning them. Iain reckoned the guy would just come and pick them up, so we left them at his Uncles for the guy to collect!

I also remember doing a double act with Iain at the Castlebay hotel in Barra. Iain was singing and doing impersonations and I was on the guitar. The lounge was in an uproar as Iain went through his repertoire of Andy Stewart, Jimmy Stewart, Tommy Cooper, Al Jolson and a host of others.

Harry Morris
Comment from Martha

My first meeting with Harry Morris was away back in 1975 when we were both Police officers in the old South Division of City of Glasgow Police. I was based in Gorbals and Harry was in Craigie Street. Our paths crossed infrequently but you could not fail to remember meeting Harry!

I was a wee rookie and Harry had a couple of years service then.

I still remember his sense of humour and his zest for fun and it was no surprise to me that he went on to make a new career as a writer. When I read his books I am transported back to my days on the beat in Gorbals. It was a tough job then for a woman but also great fun. If you read his books, you will get a clear grasp of what I mean!

I was helping Iain one day to tidy up his house, when I came across one of Harry's business cards.

"How do you know Harry?" I asked Iain.

Now…My first thought was that Harry had arrested Iain. Some Sister I was, immediately thinking the worst! Not for one moment did I think that they met in a professional capacity.

Iain went on to tell me the story of how he met Harry and what a great time they had filming together.

He had kept his card for a number of years and held Harry in high esteem. Little did I know then how instrumental Harry would be in assisting with the completion of Iain's story?

I told Iain of how I had met Harry when we were both in the Police and we agreed it was indeed a small world.

I met up with Harry not long after Iain died, explaining to him what I was tasked to do by Iain. The whole responsibility was overwhelming me and I was still struggling with losing Iain in July 2013.

Harry offered immediate support, guidance, enthusiasm and encouragement. Without his help I think I would have floundered and given up. I didn't want to let Iain down.

Thank you Harry Morris.

Harry (The Polis) Morris

I had the privilege of meeting and working with one of Scotland's Great characters and a distinguished actor, Iain McColl.

The meeting came about whilst filming in Pitlochry, Scotland on the set, when performing several TV commercials for Johnny Walker Whisky.

As it was, I was fortunate to be represented by the same "Agency" in Glasgow when I was chosen by the client, along with Iain, for the parts, this job also included an excellent piece of filming, previously recorded by Robert Carlyle, to coincide with our sketches. It was a personal thrill for me, not just being involved, but to also be working with Ian McColl and finding him to be very humble and modest when introducing himself, was something unexpected, considering his CV of TV, Stage and Film Work.

'Hello!' He said, extending his hand out to shake mine. 'You must be Harry the Polis! I'm Iain McColl... Ah hope you left your truncheon and handcuffs at home!'

This was a light-hearted reference to his troublesome and highly publicised past, but those days were well and truly long gone, this was a revitalised new man who had left his wild reputation, firmly behind in the past.

Here before me stood a true celebrity who was nothing like the wild man image of stage and screen that I had read about in the tabloids several years before. It was a pleasant meeting for me and an added bonus to be working with someone, immaterial of his well publicised past, but someone whose work I had truly respected from afar, having seen numerous performances on TV and stage and was always thoroughly impressed with his great acting ability and dedication to detail. Forget all the negative stuff that was written. His portrayal of the Legendary Chic Murray was a prime example of his undoubted talent and the ability he possessed, watching him take on the role of one of Scotland's finest comedian/actors was nothing short of fascinating and superbly performed as he went about his craft, capturing every detail, facial expression, action and voice of the immortal Chic Murray to perfection.

Not an easy task to tackle, performing one of the highly regarded greats of stage and screen, but a challenge which Ian relished and dealt with impeccably, making each and every scene, seem like a stroll in the park, for not only did he sound like him, but he even looked like him.

Forgive me for digressing but, thinking back to it, I tend to get carried away with how good he really was, but back to my story and involvement, In particular the diverse roles we had to perform on the day, the first was that of two, typical Scottish Gamekeepers, socialising, standing at a public bar, sipping away on their favourite tipple of Johnny Walker Whisky, whilst ad-libbing some hilarious Scottish "gags" to one and other, before laughing openly at each other's attempt at spontaneous humour and joke telling. However, I have to admit to laughing hysterically at times to Iain's wonderful sense of humour and his delivery, which I thoroughly enjoyed, along with the film crew involved with each scene, and I even laughed wholeheartedly when he remarked, totally out of the blue during one scene,
"'Bye the way, I saw one of your books the other day there in a shop, couldn't put it down.....I see you're still putting superglue on the covers!"

Such was the fun and laughter we were generating, the crew continued filming more scenes than was considered necessary for the shoot.

The entire episode of events and the Whisky theme was also a huge test for Iain, a self confessed alcoholic, when faced with the task, after each joke, of being told, we were expected to raise our large Whisky glasses filled with the Real Johnny Walkers product and sip on it! But like the true professional he was, he carried out the action impeccably, simulating the action, but without tasting a drop!

Next on the agenda that afternoon was the cartoon characters they were using in another TV Commercial which involved a cow, a sheep and a mouse.

"I think I'll leave you guys to work out what you want to do with these voice overs!"

Said the Director, impressed with our earlier scenes which had the entire crew laughing uncontrollably.

"What do you think big man, any ideas?"

I asked Iain.

Iain paused for a moment, then said,

"Why don't I be like a ghost like character voice, slow and precise, like Lurch from the Adams Family and you be a fast talking 'whiz kid' character voice, like a Bart Simpson, only with that broad Glaswegian accent you have, thereby creating totally different personalities entirely! I really think it will work."

"Ok with me."

I replied, taking his advice and expertise into the part.

Need I tell you, the Director and crew were delighted with what he rehearsed between us and we sailed through the parts in one "take."

It was a perfect choice of character voices, coupled with the experience of Iain coming up with the idea for the parts.

I have to admit to having a brilliant days filming with a truly brilliant Scottish actor whom I befriended from that day onwards; and kept in touch with him. He was a man who made himself readily available to give invaluable advice to a novice like myself when asked for help.

Sadly for us all, was the untimely passing of Ian after a short illness, depriving his family, friends and colleagues of stage and screen that we didn't get the chance to sample more of his undoubted humour, talent and acting ability which he possessed in abundance.

Just ask anyone who worked with him!

Iain McColl was a big man in more ways than one and a person I am proud to have known worked with and can happily call my friend.

When will we see your likes again!
Thanks for the memory Iain.

Ian Pattison

I first met Martha Brindley at her brother Iain's funeral. The month was July, the day was sunny and the service as pleasant as the nature of such occasions can allow. We wondered what Iain would have made of it all. He wouldn't have wanted to waste a good audience. If he hadn't been otherwise engaged he'd have sat up and given us his Tommy Cooper impression.

Martha told me she planned to carry out her brother's wish and finish off the book he had been writing about his life and times. She asked if I had particular memories of Iain. Oddly, I didn't know Iain at all well in his big telly days of City Lights and Rab C Nesbitt but over his last couple of years he and I would meet up occasionally for coffee – yes I do mean coffee – and would shoot the breeze. I knew Iain was recovering from serious illness at that point. If asked, he would speak about it but I took my cue from him and if he didn't care to dwell on the subject then nor would I. He was keen to work and was continuing to do so.

Iain, as is well documented, could be his own worst enemy and while there is no doubt that he was wired slightly differently from most of humanity, on a one to one basis I found him to be an intelligent and thoughtful individual with a nice line in droll humour. I remember asking him how he got into show business and he told me a tale about turning up to do some repair work at a club in Glasgow and overhearing from the manager that the male stripper booked for the evening had cancelled. Iain stepped into the breach, offering his services with the assurance that 'I served my time as a male stripper' as if he'd done a five year City and Guilds apprenticeship on how to peel off a spangled G string.

Iain appeared to have his demons under control, had reconciled with his family and was looking forward to an enjoyable third act to his life when his illness recurred. You know the outcome of that circumstance which was why Martha and I ended up standing outside the church in Knightswood, talking about Iain's book. Martha explained that Iain had been so thankful for the treatment and care he'd received at the Beatson clinic in Glasgow that he wanted all profits from the sale of his book to go there.

A lot of people talk about writing a book but for one reason or another, don't complete the task. Martha isn't one of them. She was determined from the outset to carry out her brother's wish. And she has.

Ian Pattison June 2014

Iain appearing as "Dodie" in Rab C. Nesbitt.
I love the moustache!!!

June Toner's Capers.
Big Iain 'Cool the beans' McColl

Iain was a larger-than-life character who entered my life when I was 19. The first time we met was at Marie Martin's Darnley flat… Iain's second stop on his return from the rigs… his first stop providing him a large lump of hash, small segments of which he popped into our mouths on arrival at Darnley!

I can't remember why we were at Marie's in the middle of the day, but on day one of meeting Iain I realised he was unique, as he held court that afternoon and continued to do so for years to come.

A few months into our friendship, Iain dropped by one December day to say "hello"… three days later he was still there, having taken up residence on my couch for the duration. Day four, Iain walked me to an interview at the Southern General… I started work as a Medical Secretary soon after, his infectious confidence having rubbed off.

One night around March '78 myself, Big Iain and Tania Silver got the 53 bus from Linthouse to Watt Bros. For the entire walk along Sauchiehall Street, Iain recited one Chick Murray joke after another. As we neared the Amphora Bar, Tania & I stopped to look in the window of a swish Italian furniture store, one we often dreamed of shopping in… someday.

We were aware of someone having approached Iain from behind us but were engrossed in the latest Italian designs that filled the window. Once gone, he told us who the guy was as we continued on our way to the Amph… Iain had been reciting one-liners, and Chick Murray, himself having a stroll along Sauchiehall Street, overheard and delivered the punch line. Iain had a huge grin on his face for the rest of the night.

We spent a lot of time in the Amphora, His Nibs, The Griffin, The Maggie and the Dial Inn, where Iain often came with us to see Dead Skunk…. one of the first tribute bands whose sets consisted mostly of Dr Hook & Shel Silverstein covers. The Music scene in Glasgow at that time was impressive and there was always a worthwhile gig going on somewhere in the city.

I'd met Iain through my neighbour Margaret Adams, whose friend & colleague at The Mars Bar was Marie Martin. Marie was seeing Joe Greenan, who played bass with Buckshot and the rest is history.

Iain, Tania & I would take the 57 bus from town after a night at the Amphora and head to Marie's where the band would congregate after a gig. Quite often we'd go to their gigs; where on one occasion Iain performed a striptease at an East end social club. I'd been there since the afternoon, probably having plunked college, and Iain did his thing… I think something happened that saw us all get chucked out later that evening. Nothing too crazy… maybe just lit up a spliff.

Tania lived with her mother, brother & Sister in a flat overlooking the park on Alexandra Parade. Iain often came to parties there after a city pub crawl on occasions when her mother & siblings were gone for the weekend.

On one of those nights, everyone had fallen asleep… or passed out, more like, so Iain & I (die-hards that we were) sat up talking, Bad Company playing quite low in the background, as we quietly conspired how best to use what hash, tobacco & rolling papers we had left. We decided that in my role of 'appointed joint builder', I would build the biggest joint possible with the 12 'skins' we had left. We modelled this on the giant cigarette paper insert found in 'Big Bamboo', a wildly funny Cheech & Chong album. So I set to work… 4 skins long by 3 skins wide, we filled the thing with all the cigarette tobacco we could find and the remaining hash, which was a considerable amount by any standards. As I set to work, we sat giggling very quietly for fear of waking anyone up, but as the joint neared completion, we just couldn't contain ourselves... it was the biggest joint we'd ever seen in our lives! We set about smoking it, very unsuccessfully at first, as the thing kept going out. Undeterred we kept at it, but as people started to wake up one by one, we were forced to share and to be honest, I think we were relieved.

That morning there wasn't a single bit of food in the house and the six or seven people remaining by breakfast time were pretty ravenous... obviously due to a combination of all night fasting and a severe attack of the munchies!

So Iain & I headed to the little grocer cum newsagent just downstairs from the first floor flat. We surreptitiously walked around the store, Iain setting the example by stuffing tins of beans and packs of potato scones up his duke... he was wearing a zippered bomber-style jacket, so the items sat quite nicely, held in by the waistband, though making him look about 5 months pregnant and at one point a tin of beans slipped out and hit the floor. Undeterred, we carried on with our mission. We had enough coppers to pay for Morton's rolls, but managed to pilfer bacon, eggs, beans & potato scones between us. Everyone back at the party was grateful for a huge morning nosh up, although Iain and I felt bad about ripping off the poor shop owner, but we had no choice as we were hungry and pretty skint on that particular day.

The next visit to Alexandra Parade, probably two or three weeks later, Iain & I went back to the store & told the guy we owed him for some 'borrowed' goods. We gave him enough to cover the cost and our conscience was restored.

There are so many great memories of Iain, it's hard to remember them all, but another that stands out is a visit to the Kelvin Hall,

Glasgow, when Iain, me, Tania, Jim Gaffney & his crazy pal, Bruce, from London found us at the carnival. Having exhausted as many of the rides as we could handle, Iain coerced us into a Highland fling of sorts, just underneath the Big Wheel... we drew a lot of looks from passing crowds, but Iain took on a kind of Tommy Cooper role, always the entertainer & raising a lot of laughs.

Sometimes on a Friday night, several friends, including Iain, would come back to my place from the Amphora for a 'Tiswas' party. We'd wait up all night, or catch a little sleep and wake in time for the madness that was 'Tiswas' with Chris Tarrant and the gang.

Passing the time until morning, we'd listen to Peter Cook & Dudley Moore's 'Derek & Clive Live' & Cheech & Chong for hours on end... sometimes I thought we'd die laughing! I'd also acquired an illegal recording of Shel Silverstein's 'Freakin' at the Freaker's Ball' from Tommy, the hippy & resident maintenance man at Linthouse Housing Association. Iain absolutely loved this album and we'd laugh till we cried at the crazy, outrageous lyrics. Other favourites of Iain (and the rest of us) were Dr. Hook (esp 'Sleeping Late'), Frankie Miller's 'Full House', Rumours & Dark Side of the Moon... we wore these albums out!

Spring '79, my mother paid one of her yearly visits to my brother in Holland, where he lived... I had my own place in Linthouse, but my mother's place was bigger and well suited for a decent party. This particular one took place on a Saturday night and by party standards, it was up there with some of the best... Iain's cousins Donny & Mick MacNeil were there, Joe Greenan, Matt Dunn, Margaret, Marie, Tania and a few friends from the Amphora. At around midnight two Police officers came to the door, refused our invitation to join the party (with a smile) and asked that we "turn the music down"... this we did, but as time went on, I'm sure the volume crept up a little, so that by around 2am the Police were back at the door. This time they insisted that we "turn the music off"... which we did. However, my mother had a piano and various other instruments, including a set of bongo drums. Each time the Police had come we all remarked at how lucky not to have our smoking habits discovered. But throwing caution to the wind, Mick ended up on the piano and Donny on the bongos whilst we all enjoyed what must have been a fairly riotous sing along... what a truly great party it was, on reflection.

The previous year, my mother had the wall separating the living room & bedroom recesses demolished, creating a large kitchen area that could be accessed from both front and back rooms. There was a sliding door into the bedroom, but during times of entertaining, the door would be left open allowing for a conga to travel from the living room, through the kitchen, into the bedroom, out into the hallway and back into the living room... on this particular night, during the period between the second & third visits by the local Govan Constabulary we did one such conga with Iain leading the way.

The noise level must have become unbearable for my mother's neighbours (well aware she was in Holland for the week), so at around 4.30am about ten Police Officers in total stormed the ground floor flat at No. 3 Drive Road and emptied the place. Three or four Panda Cars sat around the cul-de-sac, along with a Transit 'pick-up' van, which Iain and I were very unceremoniously thrown into. I always thought Iain had come to my defence and got apprehended as a result but I found out on the day of his service this year that it was me who objected to his treatment. He'd been joking around with the officers (probably telling them to "cool the beans") trying to raise a giggle and lighten the situation when things turned potentially nasty. I then got shirty with the officers telling them to back off and release Iain, all the while complaining they didn't have a warrant to enter the flat... there was a lot of alcohol consumed that night and I should have kept quiet. Nevertheless, and we still don't understand why, no one got busted!

Accounts from friends left behind as Iain & I headed for the slammer, were of being told to go home, though Tania and her boyfriend (& ex-Policeman) were allowed to remain since I'd have been locked out otherwise. As everyone started to disperse, Mick was playing little notes on his synthesizer, (went everywhere with him at the time) and there was frost on the ground that appeared like diamonds to one guest tripping on acid... the scene was one of dejection at the 'party of the year' being disrupted.

Standing beside Iain at the Bar in Orkney Street (we were the only 2 arrested and charged with Breach of the Peace) I was trying to focus on the clock above the duty officer noting our details, when I said "But officer, it's only 25 past 12". He said, "Dear, I think you'll find its 5 o'clock in the morning! We were thrown into individual cells and sent to court Monday morning. Iain, Donny, Mick & Joe all chipped in and paid my £25 fine... they were real sweethearts.

Around 2007/8 Plantation Productions in Govan did a film about Orkney Street jail, gathering filmed anecdotes from people who'd been banged up through the years for one misdemeanour or another. The crew came to my place where they filmed Iain & I telling our side of the story, then onto 3 Drive Road, where we described the scene as we spilled onto the street that night.

At Iain's service in Maryhill, Joe asked his brother if he remembered me. We both agreed we'd never met, when he said "I only ever met a lassie in Linthouse that had the party that got raided". I didn't even know Joe's brother had been there... and neither did Joe!

This all sounds a little crazy, but we were pretty level-headed most of the time... all keeping down jobs and living normal lives (more or less) Monday to Friday.

But there was a wind of change around that time... the Amphora was raided shortly after my infamous party, leaving us feeling like orphans with our local no longer there. Around then, we started frequenting the Mars Bar a lot more. We saw 'Jonny & the Self-Abusers' there one night, Mick's second gig with Jim Kerr & Co before they became Simple Minds.

Around that time I fell in love with someone outwith the circle, so gradually settled into a sort of domestic bliss.
I didn't see much of Iain after that, from just prior to his enrolment at Drama school, or during the height of his fame which saw him on various TV shows, but I did bump into him at the BBC when I started work there in the late-80s... we met up at Curlers that evening and had a giggle at the twist of fate bringing us back together at the BBC... it seemed a long way from our crazy days in Darnley and the Amphora.
We didn't see much of each other again until around Spring 2005, after which I saw a lot of him. I'd written a part in a short film for Iain, but kept putting it off due to work commitments. If I ever have the opportunity to actually shoot the film, it'll be dedicated to him.

In October 2005 I brought him back a Red Fez from Marrakesh, which he wore for a Tommy Cooper night at Broomhill Baptist Church. Iain was such a natural entertainer, he brought tears of laughter to everyone ... he only ever really wanted to make people laugh and would shun depressing chit-chat or news, in favour of keeping up-beat. On my 50th birthday, Iain gave me an issue of SAGA magazine, with the inscription:

Happy Birthday June!

Welcome to the Saga Generation!

Love, Iain

I near split my sides! On the cover was a great photo of Julie Andrews aged about 20 and looking fab. Iain had no idea how much I loved watching her films in the 60s, but he obviously considered my welfare when picking this gift as it contains some great pension advice & sound dietary tips for the ageing alimentary tract!

Throughout the time I knew Iain, he often shared memories of Barra and South Uist. I can't remember details; just that he loved both places and seemed to have a real attachment to them.
The last time I saw Iain was around Spring 2012 at Anniesland... he was so happy to show me his doo cat in the living room cupboard. The cupboard was filled with shelves & rows of pigeons and a lot of droppings that I said could be bad for his health, but that I thought what he was doing was fantastic... I didn't want to be completely negative about it.
He then told me his plan to get a donkey for the back green and provide local kiddies with donkey rides... he really just wanted to spread the joy!

Christmas 1977, just before my son's 3rd birthday, Iain bought Jason a pair of Kickers… Navy Blue, leather and properly fitted by Clarks. Jason was so proud of his new shoes and wouldn't wear anything else, till he could no longer get the things on. Jason loved big Iain.

The last time I spoke to Iain was in February this year, 2013. I'd had such a strong urge to call him, but kept getting side-tracked with work. When I saw Joe at the end of January he told me Iain had been in hospital. So I called him around the point he got home and promised to come see him the following week… again I let work get in the way and never did see him again.

I have some great memories of Iain and when I think of him… every day… I can't help but smile… he was a lovely big pal!

Scary Iain

Iain looking wild and mental! Restless Natives 1985

Reflections from Joe Greenan

Joe Greenan was friends with Iain for over 40 years. Iain always said that Joe was his **"Brother by another Mother."** I guess that makes you mine too Joe! Joe has always been part of our extended family and a much loved friend.

The first time I met Iain, I was playing in a group with his Cousins Donnie and Mick MacNeil in the Polmadie club. They told me their big cousin was coming. I didn't know what to expect but he came to the gig and he was jumping about daft as usual.

He had a car with him and it was in the middle of winter with two foot of snow on the ground. Iain offers to give me a run home and after the gig, we piled into the car. Iain has a burst tyre on the car and he starts off going up Victoria Road. Chuggety chug all the way along. The following day we were going to an audition for "New Faces". We reached the hill at Battlefield and the car starts spinning round in circles all the way down the hill. Iain calmly turns to us and said "Yep. It will be new faces you're getting right enough". Now Iain never had a driving licence then and we got stopped by the Police at Kennishead Road. The Police officer said to Iain "You need to get that fixed. Just make sure you don't hit anything on your way home". We did make it home safe, despite the weather and burst tyre!

I was playing a gig with Mick and Donnie in St Robert's Church hall in Peat Rd, Glasgow. Now this was in front of the Women's Guild at the request of the Parish Priest.

Iain got a bass guitar, which he couldn't play, and suspended it from a pair of old fashioned gent's braces, the ones used to hold up trousers. He played this guitar, which was bouncing up and down, from behind the stage curtain! He never tuned it up and when I asked him to tune it he just said "what for?" He spent the first half of the gig bouncing up and down behind the stage curtains.

Every so often he would peek round from the curtain playing the guitar while it was suspended by the braces round his neck! The women loved his contortions and the demented guitar playing. Nobody ever knew that Iain could not play a single note!

On another occasion, we were in the Perthshire Club in Springburn Road doing a wee gig. Iain would often come about with us to various gigs in the van. We were playing at a ladies night and they had hired a stripper from Edinburgh. This guy came out with a bouffant hairdo, hairy chest and a medallion round his neck. He was swanning about here there and everywhere.

Iain watched for a while and then said to the manager, "I can do that". The manager said he could give it a go. So Iain turned up the following week with a brown suit, shirt and tie as Mr Young Executive. It was more like a comedy routine than a strip show. He goes out on stage and starts taking his clothes off to music, wrapping the tie round and through his legs and having a right carry on. The women are going mad and Iain takes off all his kit right down to his underpants. The first pair have "**home of the big one**" written on them and then he had another four pairs on with various slogans printed. As he is the Young Executive, he has an umbrella with him on stage. He took off the last pair of pants and popped up the umbrella between his legs! The place is in an uproar and Iain went down a bomb!

The whole thing was hilarious and he brought the house down.

You think that striptease is a wee bit seedy but it wasn't like that. It was The Full Monty before it was thought of! The manager booked him again for another couple of months but Donnie and Mick never told him! Iain was going a bit off his head with depression and Bipolar and he could be a bit unreliable. He somehow had the date in his head and he turned up on the night as we were playing a gig! All the women were there waiting for Young Executive and his brolly. They were like a baying crowd looking for blood. Iain had a cowboy hat on and he's chatting up all the cowgirls! He never told his mother about the new career as Annie would have been mortified at her big son taking his clothes off in public.

So a few years later, Iain and I went off on a trip to Greece. We went down to London and met up with Simple Minds. This was in the early 70's and they were just starting out. They were playing to crowds of a couple of hundred. That was the start of our holiday. We bought a Transalpine Pass which took us through France, Italy and then on to Greece. Iain was being daft all the way there and people on boats and trains were rolling about laughing at his antics. We had a ferry journey over the Mediterranean to Greece and down to Athens. We headed off after that to an island and accumulated people along the way, two Germans, a wee lassie from Dundee and an American guy. By the time we got to the island, it was just ourselves and the two Germans. We had tents and decided to go up this mountain and find a good spot to camp. We bought a bottle of Ouzo and tanked into that with the sun beating down on us. We got a lift on a horse and cart part way up the mountain and then started walking. I fell and banged my head on a rock and got knocked out. Iain decided he was going no further and stayed halfway up the mountain camped on the track! I carried on with the Germans and it was not long before we came across a beautiful beach on the other side of the mountain. We marched down and made camp. I started shouting for Iain but he couldn't hear me. The Germans were worried about Iain and asking if "Ein" is alright. I assured them that "Ein" would be better than us!

The next morning I heard a noise coming round the mountain. "Josefo" "Josefo" and a rumble of a motorbike. There's "Ein" driving an old battered bike which someone gave to him! He went back down the mountain, found a beach bar and fell asleep at the bar. He woke up later that night to the sound of a big party going on around him. People gave him drinks and food and he had a great time. I am not too sure how he got the motorbike!

A couple of weeks later, we are leaving the island on a ferry. It was very busy with locals and donkeys, goats and chickens too!

I am sitting down on the deck and Iain starts on me. He goes into a rubbish bag and brings out an orange peel. He is shouting and a crowd gathered to watch his goings on. He shouts "touristo" and puts his finger to his head and makes a sign that I am stupid!

He drapes the orange peel round my neck like a necklace and says "necklace for touristo". He takes money out of my pocket and next he lifts a bag out of the bin. He makes it into a hat and there's me sitting with my orange peel necklace done up like a numpty! The place is in an uproar and people are laughing at our antics. Everywhere we went, Iain would make people laugh.

We next travelled by train and by the time we arrived in Italy; we were running out of money. We decided to get a pizza and a glass of milk. Neither of us could speak Italian and we ended up with a cold pizza and hot milk!

Our train was heading through France but we tried to save miles on our journey by going through Switzerland. Our tickets were not valid in Switzerland and at 3 o' clock in the morning; the ticket inspector comes to tell us we have to get off at the next station. Iain is sound asleep and I am trying to tell the inspector that we have no money left. I am worried sick but I hatch a plan. Take the train to the Swiss border and get off and walk to France along the road. Only problem was, the inspector took the tickets and passports away. We got off the train at 5am in a small town in the middle of nowhere and walked out of the station to a picture postcard Swiss town. There were chalets, mountains, cows and scenery. Iain went off, returned with a Mars bar and told me it cost £5! What a perfect place to get thrown off a train. We fell asleep on a bench for a couple of hours before being wakened by an inspector who handed back our tickets and passports. We had to sign a paper agreeing to pay the money we owed; Iain never paid me a penny!

Another time we were hanging around Darnley. I was seeing this girl at the time and after the gig, we would go back to her house. She had a young son who was about 8 years old and he was not too happy about all these weekend visitors. I woke up during the night and raided the fridge for a drink. I lifted a bottle of limeade and took a swallow. "That's pee" I said to Iain, try it. He promptly takes a drink and said, "Aye your right, it is pee".

The wee boy got his own back for his interrupted sleep but I never got over Iain actually taking the drink and trying it after I told him what it was!

Iain stayed with me for a while after his marriage broke up. He always had a thing about lighting fires. He had a black and gold waistcoat that he would wear. It was long and he would go downstairs and chop up wood for the coal fire. He had a big axe and was wearing this long coat when he bumped into my neighbour. He must have been quite a formidable sight as my neighbour turned tail and ran back indoors! He told me the guy was crazy!

Iain loved his Uncle Angus James from South Uist. He was a great man and was very fond of Iain. Iain spent some lovely summers up there and he will be laid to rest on Uist.

He was a great friend and not once in over 40 years did we fall out. I miss him every day. We spent some lovely times together and he was an amazing friend who loved nothing more than to make people laugh. He was under estimated as an actor and could have done so much more.

Rest in peace.

David Mc Kay

(Actor and Director)

Iain and I were doing 2 plays written by Billy Connolly at the Pavilion theatre in Glasgow. The show was a sell out and Iain was playing a cross-dressing landlord of a flat I was to look at.

Iain opened the door in his "Hilda Ogden" pinny and head scarf, miner's tackety boots and holding a Ken Dodd tickling stick with a big broad smile on his face.
The audience wet themselves laughing! Iain would turn his smile to each tier, and more laughter. Then, when the laughter was dying down, he'd shrug his shoulders and laugh Tommy Cooper style, ha he he he, and the audience were off again, howling with laughter.

Five minutes he had them without saying a word. Pure class!

Sonia Scott Mackay

Iain was a very talented and versatile actor.

He was known for his comedy work in Rab C Nesbitt but he could play straight roles and sing too.

Iain would drop by the agency to share a cup of green tea with me. By the end of our meeting he was singing his way out the door!

It was a privilege to have represented such a great actor.

Gavin Mitchell's fond words.

What a kind, generous, funny, supportive and beautiful man your dear brother was to me.

He was a unique and incredibly underrated actor.

Ross King

I messaged Ross King in Los Angeles as he had starred in "Comfort and Joy" with Iain way back in 1984.

Ross was very encouraging and thanked me for getting in touch with him. He said it was lovely and touching that I would finish the book. What more can a Sister do with a brother like Iain?!!!

"I'll be honest Martha, the first time I met Iain I was sooo scared, until the moment he said "Hello", and then thankfully, I realised that he wasn't going to hit me! It was the first film I had ever been involved with and, as a featured extra, I was just happy to be on set.

Iain was great and made all us extras feel at home.....and he never hit me!!!"

All the very best. Ross.x

Iain with Bill Paterson in Comfort and Joy 1983

Tony Roper's Tale

Ian and I were in Panto in Motherwell. Can't recall what the panto was. But I do remember one episode with Ian that made me, the cast and the audience laugh.
We had been doing the show for about three weeks and were into the heavy part of the run.

We were all extremely tired and only adrenaline was keeping us going. There was a circus scene in it where Ian was dressed in a fake leopard skin (kinna like the Flintstones outfits) as he was meant to be the circus strong man. Ian was up the back of the stage meant to be lifting weights. I had my back to him and I delivered this line which Ian was meant to reply to, but he didn't. When I looked round Ian had fallen asleep leaning against the back wall. Someone in the audience shouted out 'DONT WAKE HIM'. I said to the audience "every body shout as loud as you can STROMBOLLI" which was his character name. On the count of three there was a roar from the audience, which wakened Ian up. He just sort of looked around him and then said 'Thanks. Is it me to speak'? The audience shouted YES and gave him a round of applause.

I do remember that Ian's Dad died then. When he got the phone call to tell him he sat next to me and painted a tear beneath his eye, but still went on and did the performance.

Hope your book does well, you're a good Sister.

Playbill from Iain's first panto

Gary Hollywood

How could we forget that smile that Iain had? It would light up a room the minute he would walk in.

Funny, talented, caring, loving, are just some of the words to describe the man I knew.

I was lucky enough to grow up on the same street as Iain. When he knew I had the bug to act, he was one of the first to give advice and guidance to myself, age 12 at the time.

I will always have fond memories of Iain as most people that Iain touched in life will have.

Let's not forget his Tommy Cooper impersonation, now that was something!!!

Forever in my heart big man

XX Gary Hollywood XX

Brian Pettifer.

I worked with Iain in London when we starred in "Government Inspector" at the Almeida Theatre in London.
Jonathan Kent was the Director at the time. Iain never did himself any favours as he missed his young family back in Glasgow.
He drove an old Bentley at the time and every weekend, after performing, he would drive back home to Glasgow stopping for a sleep on the way. I don't know how he did it but it could only be Iain!
He put himself under a lot of pressure to get back in time for the next performance and sometimes almost missed his cue!
I tried to get him to sell the car to me but he was not for selling.

He was brilliant in his part and was a kind, gentle and good actor. He could have done so much more.

The Government Inspector
When Iain was appearing in The Government Inspector, he stayed with our Aunt, Katie Anne, in London. He missed his family and would drive home to Glasgow on Saturday evenings after the performance. He would return on Monday for the performance that evening. He certainly put himself under pressure!

Cast: Iain Andrew, Kern Falconer, Tom Hollander, Kathryn Howden, Moray Hunter, Peter Kelly, Ronnie Letham, Alex Mc Avoy, Iain McColl, Ian Mc Diarmid, Stuart Mc Quarrie, Brian Murphy, Terry Neeson, Brian Pettifer, Dirk Robertson, Tom Watson.

John Murtagh and "Big Cheesy"

The big man, at times, was smart enough to play the "daftie".
One example of this was how he acquired the nickname of "Big Cheesy".
It goes like this:
As a young man, Iain worked as a scaffolder, and in those times you brought your own sandwich or "piece" as it was called in Glasgow, for your dinner break (lunch).
On the first day, Iain clocked that the older guys were really interested in what you had on your "pieces". If it was something out of the run of the mill then a swap was "suggested", or if the older guys never had a piece, then a donation was on the cards.
Iain, for the first wee while, always had cheese on his pieces, to the extent that nobody had any interest in what the contents were. He had the Mickey taken out of him for eating cheese every day, hence "Big Cheesy".
Of course, after the first few weeks of inspection, Big Cheesy switched the contents of his pieces and was able to munch away at "corn dobby" (corned beef) and all the other delicacies of his piece box.

"I don't do impressions"

When Iain was being Tommy Cooper in the play "Waiting for Tommy" by David Cosgrove, he had to do lots of publicity work for the show.
He would turn up with the fez and crack a few gags and all was well until….

Iain was doing a radio interview and said "I'm useless at doing these radio things as myself".
"No problem", I said, "Do them as Tommy Cooper".

Iain did this for about 20 minutes until the radio interviewer got a bit hacked off. He wanted to interview Iain McColl, the actor. "Right, you have convinced me you your Tommy Cooper to a tee! Now could you please let us hear Iain McColl?"

There was a slight pause, then, Iain speaking as Tommy Cooper, said "I'm sorry. I don't do impressions!"

By John Murtagh.

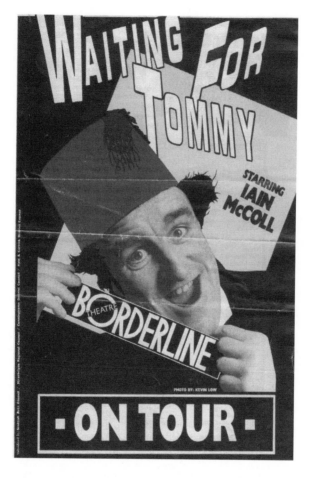

PLAYBILL FROM IAIN'S "TOMMY COOPER"TOUR
Iain was amazing in this role, the resemblance was incredible

Iain as Tommy Cooper

Alex Norton

Alex Norton informed me of the last time he spoke with Iain and he reminded Alex of the time they worked together on COMFORT AND JOY.

He confided to Alex that he was uncertain about his future in the business. Alex told him that with his unique looks; he would never be out of work for very long...

Iain appearing in Taggart as a barman.

John Stahl

I was very sad to hear of Iain's passing, but it does not surprise me at all that he was entertaining his fellow patients up till the end.

I worked with Iain only the once, on a play for 7:84 called "Beneath One Banner," which toured Scotland in 1987. A story about the Orange and the Green set in the East of Scotland. Iain played the father of a family of Irish immigrants who'd been brought over from Ireland at the time of The Great Famine to work the mines outside Edinburgh and to take the jobs from Scottish miners who were on strike at the time.

My memories of Iain's performance were the power he brought to his characterisation. He was well known at that time for his comic performances on television but I don't think the audience were prepared to see how good a straight actor he was. It always saddened me that he never widened the range of work that he did.

However the memory that sticks with me is the first time we met. I was invited to a production of a pantomime given by the final year students at the RSAMD. Iain was playing Dame. From his first entrance to his last he had the audience eating out of the palm of his hand. We met in the pub afterwards and had a great time, jokes, stories about the business etc. And Iain was interested in any advice I could give him about how to take his career forward. I came up with what advice I could; including the fact that I said he should join Equity. At the time you could only join the union if you had work, and you had to be proposed by a member in good standing, so I said that if he wanted I would be happy to propose him for membership when the time came. We parted and that was that. Fast forward a couple of weeks and there was I during a period of "resting", working behind the bar of a pub in Bridge of Allan and on comes Iain, large as life, Equity membership form in hand requiring my signature. This was in the days before mobile phones and we hadn't swapped home numbers, so I asked him how he'd found me. He told me that I'd mentioned Bridge of Allan in the conversation we'd had, so he'd driven to Bridge of Allan stopped the first person he'd met in the Main Street and asked where he could find Inverdarroch from Take The High Road and they'd directed him to the pub. I was more than happy to sign his form, and even happier to hang up my barman's apron and retire with him to the other side of the bar where we had an afternoon of stories and songs, and he was killing himself laughing over the fact he was about to start an acting job and I was serving drink in the pub!

Those are my memories of your brother, Martha.

A natural comedian, a strong dramatic actor and a person of great humanity with a gigantic lust for life.

John Stahl.

Colin Gilbert

Iain first came to see me just after graduating from the RSAMD, just for a meeting. He had brought with him a briefcase which I soon discovered contained a couple of props.

His first ploy was his "impression" of Elvis Presley, which involved him lying down in front of me with his arms across his chest. I thought "Oh Dear."

Next, he did his impression of Ray Charles. This involved him putting a black stocking over his head and then some sunglasses over that and singing something, I don't remember what.

"Oh Dear, Oh Dear," I thought. Coming, as I did at the time from a fairly "right on" school of comedy and fresh from working on "Not The Nine O'clock News."

Iain's look and attitude, however, made me feel he was worth a try. We were about to make the pilot for "City Lights," in 1984. There was a character in the script called "Tam" who was a big stupid eejit. I do not know why I immediately thought of Iain, but I did.

It was a huge success both for me and for Iain.

The much loved "Big Tam"

Tom Urie's story.

I met Iain once, and it was-believe it or not-at a dance workshop in the 90's.

It was run by Andy Byatt at the Actors Studio led by Stuart Hopps, the original choreographer for the Rocky Horror Picture Show.

The week long workshop involved about 12 people, all actors from different walks of life. They gave us each a role and a song to work on and we would give a performance at the end of the week.

I think I was Brad, someone else was Rif Raf....and Iain decided that he would be the transsexual lead man, Frank n' Furter.

It wasn't a public performance and, at the end of the week, we all gave our performances in front of 5 or 6 invited people.
Little did we know that Iain had planned a wee surprise!

None of us had bothered about costume-but as the opening chords to "Sweet Transvestite" started up-out came Iain in full basque, stockings and suspenders complete with full make up on!

He was fantastic, and it was such a surprise, he stole the show!

I only met him once but I thought he was a lovely guy.

Obituary (Extract from Scotsman)

Iain McColl left school with no qualifications, worked on the rigs offshore and started off in show business as a roadie and a stripper, before going on to become one of the most familiar faces in Scottish television comedy.

In the 1980s and early 1990s he played Big Tam in the Glasgow sitcom City Lights, with Gerard Kelly and Andy Gray. And he was Rab's none-too-bright drinking buddy Dodie in around 40 episodes of the BBC's hugely successful comedy Rab C Nesbitt, with Gregor Fisher as the Govan anti-hero, in the 1990s.

On screen McColl could bring new depth and passion to the whole concept of glaikit. His heartfelt rendition of A Wee Cock Sparra, for Scottish Television's Hogmanay special in 1990, invited and stood comparison with the great Duncan Macrae.

McColl was also a gifted mimic and his impression of Tommy Cooper was legendary. And he shared something of Cooper's slightly different take on reality.

He was back at the King's in Glasgow in the 1990-91 pantomime Babes in the Wood, with Gerard Kelly, Rikki Fulton and Una McLean. He appeared in several Borderline Theatre Company productions and in 1997-98 he was reunited with Rab C Nesbitt co-star Brian Pettifer in London's West End, in John Byrne's adaptation of Gogol's The Government Inspector.

But it was not all funny ha-ha. He played a condemned man, awaiting the hangman's noose, in Martin Scorsese's epic Gangs of New York in 2002, alongside Leonardo DiCaprio, Daniel Day-Lewis, Gary Lewis and various other Scottish actors.

And his brushes with the law were not confined to the screen. McColl struggled with drink and drug problems and had convictions for drink-driving and assault. He spent several months in jail in 2005 for repeated drink-driving.

While many screen stars seem to shrink in the flesh, McColl was the opposite – a larger-than-life character who left an indelible impression wherever he went.

His City Lights co-star Andy Gray described him as **"slightly bonkers"**, recalling how McColl once went to an audition, wearing a fez, and did his usual perfect impression of the late Tommy Cooper – despite the fact that the role had absolutely nothing to do with Tommy Cooper.

There was a time, while he was making Rab C Nesbitt that he had no home and was living in his car – although it was a Rolls-Royce, a story that reflects both a certain degree of success and of disorganisation in his life.

His parents met while working on the Glasgow trams. Iain Patrick McColl was born in Lennox Castle Hospital on 27th Jan 1954, but grew up largely in the Kinning Park district – pretty much home territory for Rab and Dodie.

His parents were keen theatre goers and took McColl to the theatre regularly as a boy. However, he had little thought of a career on stage or screen when he left school and he worked as a roustabout on rigs in the North Sea and the Persian Gulf.

Subsequently McColl worked as a roadie and he made his stage debut, more or less by accident, when a stripper failed to turn up for an engagement and he offered to take his place. "I borrowed a suit and an umbrella and went down a bomb as Mr Executive," he later recalled.

Encouraged by Jim Kerr of Simple Minds to think about acting as a career, McColl auditioned for and got into the Royal Scottish Academy of Music and Drama in Glasgow and proved to be an outstanding student He saw his future in comedy and perfected a number of impressions, employing a fez for Tommy Cooper and pulling a black stocking over his face to add a touch of authenticity to his Ray Charles.

He was lucky that the BBC's Comedy Unit in Glasgow was just beginning to make its mark under producer Colin Gilbert, and McColl became part of the regular troupe. He featured on City Lights, in which Gerard Kelly was a teller at the fictional Strathclyde Savings Bank and McColl was one of his friends. And he was a regular on the sketch show Laugh??? I Nearly Paid My Licence Fee, with Robbie Coltrane and John Sessions.

City Lights was one of the Comedy Unit's big early hits. There were six series and a couple of theatre productions. McColl reprised his character on stage at the King's Theatres in Glasgow and Edinburgh and on tour. Rab C Nesbitt was an even bigger hit, with its colourful cast of characters acquiring a cult following throughout the UK.

The success of City Lights and Rab C Nesbitt provided McColl with regular employment throughout much of the 1980s and 1990s, but he also took on a number of other projects, both on screen and in the theatre.

On television McColl also had recurring roles on the Comedy Unit's Atletico Partick and on the fondly remembered Hamish Macbeth, in which Robert Carlyle played the eponymous laid-back Scottish Highland Policeman and McColl was "Neil the Bus".

He also had one-off roles on various other television series, including The Tales of Para Handy, The Crow Road, The Book Group, Taggart and Still Game. In 2008 he revealed he had been diagnosed with cancer, but it looked as if treatment had been successful. Rab C Nesbitt was revived that same year, and McColl returned to the role of Dodie in several episodes in 2011.

He was also linked a few years ago with plans for a film about the Scottish boxing champion Benny Lynch. McColl was to have played Lynch's trainer, but the film fell through.

McColl was divorced and is survived by three children Rhianan, Ciaran and Maurice.

Praising his comedic talents and promising to raise a glass in his memory, Andy Gray said "We were a bit of a double act in a way. We had a lot of laughs on set. We would do five-page scenes and Iain would get the big laugh at the end with just one line. He'd come in and steal it. There was nobody quite like him - he was a true character.

"We will have a drink for him and relive happy memories of our big, daft Iain. Our sadness will be tinged with a lot of laughter and funny memories but my thoughts are with his family."

City of Glasgow Halls and Theatres
Manager: WILLIAM G. DIFFER   Assistant Manager: DAVID F. McSHANE

TUESDAY 11 DECEMBER '90 — SATURDAY 23 FEBRUARY '91
Evenings at 7.00 pm   Matinees at 2.15 pm

THE CITY OF GLASGOW
presents

GERARD   IAIN
KELLY   McCOLL

in

IN THE

with
UNA McLEAN

Eric Cullen • Michael MacKenzie • Judith Hibbert
Susannah Jupp • Kenneth Lindsay
The Acromaniacs

Musical Arranger   Lighting Designer
Patrick McCann   **George Armstrong**

Book Written and Directed by
RIKKI FULTON

Musical Director   Set Designer   Costume Designer
Jill Stewart   **Len Hannibal**   **Mark Cantor**

Fight Choreographer   Staged & Choreographed by
Roger Martin   **Rhona Cleland**

135

IAIN

McCOLL
(Babe)

Iain McColl graduated from the RSAMD having won the gold medal and the comedy prize. One of his first theatre performances was as McPhail in the stage version of *Para Handy*. He has appeared as Inspector McKenzie in *The Return Of A. J. Raffles* at the Edinburgh Festival. He has worked with 7:84, Cumbernauld and Motherwell Theatre and latterly the smash hit *City Lights* tour.

He was seen in the award winning *Tumbledown* for BBC TV and he also appeared in *Knockback*, *The Holy City*, *Down Where The Buffalo Go*, *You've Never Slept In Mine*, *Rab C. Nesbitt* and most notably in *City Lights* as Big Tam.

His other television appearances include *Stookie*, *The Campbells*, *Take The High Road* and *Taggart*. Iain's film credits include *Restless Natives* and *Comfort And Joy*. He has completed two series as Mr Sinclair in *Half Way To Paradise* for Channel 4.

136

Doing what Iain did best, making people laugh

Obituary (Extract from the Herald)

Iain McColl the Dumbarton- born actor, who played Doddie in BBC sitcom Rab C Nesbitt, died at the Beatson Clinic in Glasgow where he had been undergoing chemotherapy. Today, his Sister Martha said the 59-year-old had been entertaining people until the end. She said: "Just last week he put on a show for the patients and staff at the hospital and he was hilarious.

"He was doing impersonations of Chic Murray and Tommy Cooper and he had people in stitches. He couldn't not make people laugh."

McColl was regarded as one of the funniest actors in Scotland.

During his career he worked extensively for the Comedy Unit production centre in Glasgow and starred alongside Gerard Kelly in 1980s sitcom City Lights as Big Tam.

He also had roles in films such as Gangs of New York and Comfort and Joy. And at one point he toured as a magician.

His personal life was every bit as colourful as the characters he played on screen. McColl found himself written up on Police charge sheets several times, and had a history of substance abuse.

He was banned from driving for 10 years after being found guilty of drink driving.

Sister Martha said: "He lived life at 100 miles per hour. He was like that since he was a baby."

The actor first revealed he had cancer in 2008. He had cleaned up his act and become teetotal.

It looked as though he had beaten the disease and Nesbitt writer Ian Pattison was keen to reintroduce his character back into the show.

n 2011 he returned to Rab C. Nesbitt, taking his customary place at the bar of the Five Ways pub alongside Brian Pettifer's Andra.

Martha said her brother passed away quietly in his sleep. She said: "He wasn't in any pain. He never complained during the whole time he was ill.

"He went to sleep on Wednesday night and slept right through. He passed away last night at around 9pm."

The funeral has yet to be arranged. However Martha, who was her brother's carer in the last year of his life, asked those who attend not to bring flowers.

She said: "Iain said that's not what he wanted. If people would like to make a donation to the Beatson Hospital that would be fantastic." The hospital staff are devastated. Iain made such a huge impact upon them.

"And I'd really like to say the care they gave him right to the end was fantastic."

What a wonderful obituary to my brother. My thanks go to Brian Beacom of the Glasgow Herald and also to The Scotsman for their kind words.

My Way
Thoughts from Martha

Iain often sung this song, especially in the car on the way to his chemotherapy on Thursdays. He would sing it with a cheeky grin and a twinkle in his brown eyes as he drove along Great Western Road to the Beatson. In his own way, he was trying to give me comfort during that difficult time.

And now, the end is here
And so I face the final curtain
My friend, I'll say it clear
I'll state my case, of which I'm certain
I've lived a life that's full
I travelled each and every highway
And more, much more than this, I did it my way

Regrets, I've had a few
But then again, too few to mention
I did what I had to do and saw it through without exemption
I planned each charted course, each careful step along the byway
And more, much more than this, I did it my way

Yes, there were times, I'm sure you knew
When I bit off more than I could chew
But through it all, when there was doubt

I ate it up and spit it out
I faced it all and I stood tall and did it my way.

Iain said the words just suited his personality!

Iain would often reminisce about our parents and our young years together as children. We always had lots of laughter in the car going to and from the hospital. We would have a bit of lunch and a chat before Iain departed along the corridor with a cheery wave of his hand. "Toodle oo the noo Sis", he would say as he went in to have blood taken. I would hear the nursing staff laugh at his jokes and I often wondered how he stayed so cheerful.

He certainly taught me a lot about coping with illness and facing death. He had such dignity and courage and as I looked at him my heart would be breaking in two.

I only cried once in front of Iain, when the doctor told him there was nothing more he could do for him. "Palliative Care," the words he used. I was broken hearted looking at Iain; he was very weak and thin by this time but cheery within himself. I could find no words but the doctor said "Iain, I think your Sister needs a hug". Iain then hugged me, took my hand and we walked out of the hospital. We never said a word to each other but by the time we got to the car park, Iain had me in stitches with his jokes and observation of life!

Iain always lived life in the way he felt at that moment in time.

He was always his own person and never thought about the consequences of his actions but this made him the unique person which he was. I wouldn't have had him any other way although we had many disagreements about the way he was living his life at times! We were a typical brother and Sister, always squabbling and arguing over stupid things.

Our love for each other carried on throughout our lives despite our very separate paths. He was never Iain McColl the actor to me, but always Iain, my big brother.

Iain's reputation as an actor meant everything to him. He had lost a part of it when he was drinking heavily, taking drugs and begun to gain a reputation for being unreliable. He worked hard and went on to work again with a new agent, Sonia Scott Mackay. Iain thought the world of Sonia and when I visited him a week before he died, he was feeling a bit low. He eventually told me what was on his mind. He had won a part in a film set on Mull but had to inform Sonia he was too unwell to fulfil his commitment. His only thought was, not for himself but that Sonia would think he was unreliable. I quickly reassured him that I had spoken to Sonia and she had sent her best wishes, but my heart was breaking for him

I had never seen this side of Iain before but it showed his true professionalism as an actor. He didn't like to let people down.

The same attitude he displayed the night our Dad died.

Dr Soutar's Final Words.

Multiple myeloma is a serious diagnosis to receive. Although significant, perhaps even in retrospect spectacular, improvements in survival have been achieved over the last 20 years myeloma to all extent remains a treatable but incurable cancer of the bone marrow.

Myeloma is characterised by high levels of immune proteins in the blood and an excess of the cells that produce these proteins, "plasma cells", in the bone marrow. While the plasma cells are producing too much protein they are still interacting with the bone forming cells in the bone structure. This interaction leads to the typical features of multiple myeloma in terms of bone marrow failure (generally presenting as anaemia), bone weakness, generally presenting as pain, and potentially kidney problems secondary to high protein levels in the blood.

I remember well the day that Iain first attended our Specialist Myeloma Clinic, at that time down at the Western Infirmary, in the presence of our Specialist Nurse, Lesley Stirton.

Sometimes medical treatment for cancer, particularly chemotherapy, is described as a "recipe". While this is sometimes the case treatment often has to be adjusted to the particular individual circumstances – we are all unique, and I do not think Iain would object to me saying that it was clear from the outset that this was most definitely the case with Iain.

Despite the seriousness of the diagnosis Iain appeared to take this with equanimity and a general air of acceptance. His demeanour changed little over the years that we looked after him: polite, easy to talk to but with a certain look in his eyes that was both mischievous and at the same time slightly sceptical. I think from the outset it was clear to me and Sister Stirton that there was always the potential for "other stuff" going on in the background!

Treatment for myeloma involves periods on and then off treatment, when the disease is controlled. Unfortunately, the natural history of myeloma is that although it tends to respond well to treatment it keeps coming back, sadly with increasing frequency.

Periods of treatment can be very intense involving frequent clinic attendance and, at times, hospital admission.

I do not think that Iain would object to me saying that the phrase "frequent clinical/hospital attendance" is one that did not fit well with him. Perhaps it was the island blood but there was a definite trait to **"do his own thing"**. For both medical and nursing staff this induced some "!" disquiet when, after delivery of potentially toxic treatment, the patient then seems to disappear.
I do not know if Iain had any sleepless nights about his condition but certainly this led to some cold sweats in the middle of the night in the medical and the nursing staff caring for him.

However, over time we learned that Iain would come back to us and importantly that he took the responsibility for this approach upon himself. From a medical point of view "mutual trust" is an important phrase when you are dealing with a long term, serious and eventually fatal condition like myeloma. For better or worse it is your life, your illness and up to you how you want to play the game. Autonomy is so important; the hospital is a hospital, not a prison.

As a doctor I tend not to read the paper but from time to time I would notice while passing a newsstand Iain's picture on the front of a paper and a description of the battles he was fighting. We

144

never discussed this but I was always extremely grateful and appreciative of the fact that he kept our names out of the press. That is the kind of attention that is not welcomed by medical or nursing staff, as he clearly appreciated.

Perhaps Iain had a "celebrity lifestyle" but in his dealings with medical and nursing staff he was always polite, courteous and gentle.

As time went on the battle got harder and the climb to clinical recovery more difficult. Finally the glint that was always present in Iain's eye began to wane. I am pleased that we could keep him on our ward in the Beatson, comfortable in the final phase of his illness. He died surrounded by his family, in peace and with the "Vatersay Boys" playing in the background. That is how he would have wanted it.

Iain was certainly a very memorable patient. The treatment bought him extra years of life which I am sure he lived to the maximum, and in his own way.

I am grateful to his Sister, Martha, for her permission to release the above information.

We miss Iain at clinic.

Iain's final journey.

Iain's wish was for his remains to be taken to South Uist and so we made a last trip to the island he loved so much.

On the eve of the service, 2nd July 2014, I walked with my dog on the Machair at Garrynamonie my thoughts were far away.
I pondered on growing up having Iain as a brother. Life was certainly always eventful and rarely dull!

The sun was beating down and I sat on a rock, remembering Iain as a child scampering along the shore.
I looked across to Orasay Island and watched Donny, my younger brother, with his son Calum, walking across to the island.

Iain loved Uist and its people with all his heart and I was not surprised when he asked me to bring his ashes to be interred there. Uist is where he was at peace with his demons and close to his beloved Uncle Angus James.

My mind was overflowing with memories and as I looked over the Atlantic Ocean, I felt a sense of peace come over me.
I could hear Iain's voice in my head saying:
"Come on Mana! Run to Orasay with me. You can't catch me!"
His brown eyes were twinkling and I could hear his laughter.
Iain called me Mana when he was a child as he couldn't get his tongue round the "r" in my name.

I prayed for my Mother, Father and Iain, hoping that they were at peace.

Iain's ashes were interred in Hallan Cemetery on 3rd July after a beautiful service in Garrynamonie Church. Family and friends were in attendance to say goodbye.

Iain, I did it "your way!"

Filmography

A Little Bit of Knowledge Is a Dangerous Thing (Short)
- Ferguson (voice)

1990-2011 - Rab C. Nesbitt (TV Series) - Dodie
- Stool (2011) - Dodie
- Role (2011) - Dodie
- Broke (2011) - Dodie
- Trips (1999) - Dodie
- Bug (1999) - Dodie

2008 - Fuming (Short)
Narrator

2007 - Still Game (TV Series)
Charlie the Lollipop Man
- Christmas Special: Plum Number (2007) - Charlie the Lollipop Man

2006 - Driving Lessons
Policeman

2003 - Taggart (TV Series)
Roy Skeen
- Atonement (2003) - Roy Skeen

2002 - Gangs of New York
Seamus - Condemned Man (as Iain McColl)

2002 - The Book Group (TV Series)
Taxi Driver 2
- The Alchemist (2002) - Taxi Driver 2 (as Ian McColl)

1996-1997 - Hamish Macbeth (TV Series)
Neil the Bus
- More Than a Game (1997) - Neil the Bus
- Radio Lochdubh (1996) - Neil the Bus
- Isobel Pulls It Off (1996) - Neil the Bus
- A Perfectly Simple Explanation (1996) - Neil the Bus

1996 - Gadgetman (TV Movie)
Lonnie Dolan

1996 - The Crow Road (TV Mini-Series)
Undertaker - Prentice (1996)– Undertaker

1996 - Atletico Partick (TV Series) - Pettigrew
- Final (1996) - Pettigrew
- Gartcosh (1996) - Pettigrew
- Girlfriends (1996) - Pettigrew
- Dropped (1996) - Pettigrew
- Balance (1996) - Pettigrew

1994 - The Tales of Para Handy (TV Series)
MacDonald
-The End of the World (1994) - MacDonald

1993 - I, Lovett (TV Series)
Policeman
- Crime & Punishment (1993) - Policeman

1984-1991 - City Lights (TV Series)
Tam
- The Haunting of Willie Melvin (1991) - Tam
- Episode 6.6 (1991) - Tam
- Episode 6.5 (1991) - Tam
- Parenthood (1991) - Tam

- Unhealthy Competition (1991) - Tam

1990 - The Campbells (TV Series)
Dougal
- Old Ways and New (1990) - Dougal

1988 - Tumbledown (TV Movie)
Colour Sergeant

1987 - The Houseman's Tale (TV Mini-Series)
Billy the steward
- Episode 1.2 (1987) - Billy the steward
- Episode 1.1 (1987) - Billy the steward

1985 - Restless Natives
Nigel

1984 - Comfort and Joy
Archie

Iain looking pensive.

The following lyrics are from a favourite song of Iain's, sung by the Vatersay boys & was played as a recessional at his Funeral Service at the Crematorium.

Road to Vatersay

Last night while I was walking, I saw a falling star
And I wished upon that star that you were near.
I wished that I could hold you every single day
And I wished upon that star that you were here.

Will we ever be together, like a flower in the rain?
Will you ever hold my hand and walk along the pure white sands….On the road,
On the road to Vatersay.

Maybe I'm on your mind, Maybe I'm in your dreams.
Maybe that's just the way it seems to me.
We could be together for all eternity.
And live our lives in perfect harmony.

Will we ever be together? You're a million miles away.
Will you ever hold my hand and walk along the pure white sands…on the road.
On the road to Vatersay.

Iain slipped away peacefully, holding my hand.
The final words I said to him were in Gaelic.
"Oidhche Mhath Ma Tha!

Goodnight.
You were the most amazing and talented big brother.
Frustrating and difficult to live with, your own unique person
and certainly very much loved by your family.

Here's tae us, wha's like us?
Damned few .....And they're a' deed